GLENN JOH

DEC 2003

PRAISE FOR TAKE ME TO YOUR LEADER$

"Information Technology solutions are a major change for an organization and impact everyone. CIO's, CFO's CEO's and other C's initiate, influence and approve these decisions. *Take Me To Your Leader$* stepped me through an effective process of establishing useful relationships with these executives."
—**Robert W. Johnson**, VP and General Manager, North America Sales and Services, Unisys Corp.

"Selling foundry services to leading edge semiconductor companies requires being positioned with the corporate leaders. *Take Me To Your Leader$* is right on target for getting powerful executives feeling comfortable with TSMC and turning decisions our way."
—**Dr. Kenneth Kin**, Senior VP, Worldwide Marketing and Sales, Taiwan Semiconductor Manufacturing Company, Ltd.

"*Take Me To Your Leader$* showed me that existing contacts in high places can be a revenue machine for our people. Sam lays-out the steps to keep our Golden Networks alive and productive."
—**Glen Edgerly**, Director Sales Training and Development, Emerson Process Controls

"Selling advanced technology into mature markets requires changes that only the senior executives will initiate. Getting to these leaders and getting to an understanding of what we can do for each other is what *Take Me To Your Leader$* is about."
—**Mike Roppolo**, Vice President Sales, FieldCentrix

"*Take Me To Your Leader$* presents the credibility map for getting senior executives to believe you can deliver the results they need to succeed. Once they feel this way, price and all other issues get solved right away."
—**Barry Rapozo**, President, Tokyo Electron of America

A Salesperson's Perspective

What's unique about *Take Me To Your Leader$* is that it gets salespeople, like me, to believe we belong with powerful, senior executives. Once I felt this confidence, I became a laser to the executive suite. If this makes you uncomfortable, learn as I did. **There is a way** to feel that these busy achievers want to see *you*, the expert who will help them. **There is a way** to get-to these decision-makers without alienating subordinates and **there is a way** to develop close, professional relationships with the people that control the company and the decisions.

Everybody knows that if you have access to the C's and other senior managers, you have a significant advantage. So why is it that we have so few accounts where we are frequently talking directly with high level people?

It's because:
- We're blocked from these movers and shakers.
- If we do get to them, they are anxious to get rid of us.
- Then, even if they do talk and listen to us, we never really connect.
- Finally those who did work well with us in the past are no longer there for us.

Most of us encounter these problems and find ourselves stuck with the subordinates who have little power.

This book will work us through dynamic solutions to these issues. It shows why obstacles arise and how to avoid or turn them around. It provides tools to use when confronted with each of these problems. It reveals the strategies, tactics, and techniques that the most successful salespeople use.

Finally, *Take Me To Your Leader$* provides the **skills** and the **emotional intelligence** to be seen as competent, confident, and creditable. Then, executives will want to see you, want to talk with you, and want to do business with you, over and over again.

TAKE ME TO YOUR LEADER$

A Step by Step
System to
Substantially
Increase Sales
by Establishing Executive Relationships

Samuel G. Manfer

ALMERSA Publishing • California

Published by: ALMERSA Publishing
20 Richmond Hill
Laguna Niguel, CA 92677, USA
info@ALMERSApublishing.com

TAKE ME TO YOUR LEADER$
A Step by Step System to Substantially Increase Sales
by Establishing Executive Relationships
Sam Manfer

ISBN 0-9722817-0-3
Library of Congress Control Number 2002093907
Printed in Canada

Publisher's Cataloging-in-Publication
(Provided by Quality Books, Inc.)

Manfer, Samuel G.
    Take me to your leader$: a step by step system to
substantially increase sales by establishing executive relationships /
by Samuel G. Manfer. -- 1st ed.
    p. cm.
    ISBN 0-9722817-0-3
    LCCN 2002093907

    1. Selling. 2 Executives. I. Title. II. Title:
Take me to your leaders
HF5438.25.M36 2002   658.85
                    QBI02-200581

Book Design by Pamela Terry, Opus 1 Design

10 9 8 7 6 5 4 3 2 1
First Printing

Table of Contents

About the Author   ix

Acknowledgments   xi

Section I – Up Close and Professional
1   Leaders Make Decisions –   17
    Subordinates Do the Legwork

2   The Sale: 21
    A Beginning, An End, and What's In-Between

3   Marketing, Selling and Executive Relationships –   23
    What You Didn't Learn in College

4   Professional Relationships, Social Relationships   29

Section II – Overcoming the Obstacles –
            Getting to the Executives
5   Obstacle 1 – Identifying the Powerful Executives   37

6   Networking, Using What Resources You Have   46

7   Leveraging – Building a Golden Network: 51
    The Info/Intro Highway

8   Obstacle 2 – Gatekeepers and Blockers   57

9   Obstacle 3 – Executive Intimidation   64

10 Obstacle 4 – You Feel the Executive Has   68
    No Time or Reason to See You

11 Obstacle 5 – The Decision Has Been Delegated.   70
    It Is Unnecessary to See the Executives

12 Obstacle 6 – You're Not at the Executives' Level   72

13 Obstacle 7 – The Embedded Competitor   74

Section III – Preparing for the Meeting

14   Credibility, The Magic of Any Relationship   **79**

15   Confidence, A Salesperson's Biggest Asset   **83**

16   Your Trinity,   **90**
      Gaining Confidence, and Overcoming
      Self-Doubt

Section IV – Talking with an Executive

17   Productive Executive Discussions   **105**

18   Asking the Questions   **111**
      That Will Provide An Arsenal
      of Powerful Information

19   Getting the Critical Information   **119**

20   Learn Their Personality Style and
      Create Great Chemistry   **127**

Section V – Forming the Relationship

21   Ingratiate the Executive   **133**
      by Using Your Arsenal of Information

22   Deliver the Expectations and Win the Executive   **138**

Section VI – Maintaining the Relationship

23   Positive Professional Impacts   **151**
      Bond the Relationship

24   Stay Involved or Your Competitor Will   **154**
      Steal Your Relationship

25   Build a Plan to Maintain the Relationship   **157**

About the Author

Sam is the principle member of Sam Manfer, Sales Consultants. He and his associates help their clients *sell more*. Sam's concepts and ideas are based on research from top sales people and his own personal experiences.

Now Sam is the author of TAKE ME TO YOUR LEADER$.

Sam received his BS in Civil Engineering and his MBA in Management Science and Marketing from the State University of New York (SUNY) at Buffalo and joined Fisher Price Toys, then a Division of The Quaker Oats Company. He coordinated the funding, design, construction and start-up of over 4,000,000 sq. ft. of manufacturing, distribution, R&D, and office space. For his accomplishments Sam received the Top Performers Award from Quaker Oats in 1975.

In 1977 Sam joined the Carborundum Company, now a Division of British Petroleum and quickly moved from Capital Engineering and Planning to Business Development. His biggest impact was taking a floundering industrial, ceramic, textile product-line and turning it into a fast growth, profitable, asbestos replacement product-line. As a result he received the Triple Threat Performance Award in 1981.

Sam then became VP of Sales and Marketing for Gemcor – a high tech, equipment integrator for the aerospace industry and quickly moved them into the automotive industry. His team designed and sold the process and all the equipment for the fabrication of the Hummer vehicle chassie to American Motors in 1982.

Then in 1984 Sam went out on his own and started to really learn how to sell. He became a manufacturers' rep and built a successful business selling factory automation components. In 1986 he opened a North American distribution company, ATP Inc. that imported and sold industrial robots. He recruited, trained and managed a channel of 15 manufacturing rep firms. As a rep and owner Sam hit the pavement selling to customers, principles and his channel partners. In 1995 he decided to pursue his passion, which is, *helping people become all they are capable of being* – the motto of his alma mater.

To do this Sam approached Miller Heiman, a prominent sales training company to learn how to be an expert in the process of selling. He quickly became a member of their Million Dollar Club which is reserved for their top sales people. It was a proud and rewarding moment when he received his $18,000 Cellini Rolex, watch.

Today Sam is a popular public speaker and a member of the National Speakers Association.

Sam's background prepared him well for this book. His formal education was coupled with his corporate experiences to make him aware of the complex business of selling. His selling skills were honed on customers' front doors and corporate executive suites. These skills were polished with coaching from some of the best salespeople in the world. Sam beams with credibility and take-it-to-the-bank believability. His concepts and thoughts are spelled-out here for your success.

Industry Experience and Partial Client List:

Computers/Technology	Apple, 3Com, Computer Assoc., Novell, Pearson Education
Engineer/Construction	CS Integrated, Fluor, IT Corp, Parsons Brinkerhoff, ProLogis
Financial/Insurance	Aon, Blue Shield, CNA, Fidelity, Health Partners, Kemper, Valic, Zurich
Healthcare	Abbott, Apria, Bergen Brunswig, Guidant, Prescription Solutions, Qiagen
HiTech/Heavy Equip	ABB, Emerson, Lam Research, Thyssen, Ultratech Stepper
Hotels/Food Services	Marriott, Sodexho
Semi Conductors	Micron, National Semi Conductor, TSMC
Telecommunications	Harris Communications, Lockheed Martin, Sprint, WorldCom
Other Industries	Corporate Express, Orange Co. *Register*, Ruan Transportation

Acknowledgments

There are many people to thank for the development of this book. My education and experiences came with the help of teachers, coaches, bosses, vendors, customers, associates, and friends. However, the major spirit, inspiration, and help came from the finite group that I thank here.

Maureen Ellen Manfer, my beautiful, ever resourceful wife of 29 years nurtured me with on-going optimism, love, and support. Maureen encouraged me to give myself permission to take the risks while she masked her fear. She continually provided the soft and welcome arms to catch me when and if the parachute didn't open. She has been a true partner and a friend. I love her.

Samantha, Meredith, and Alexis Manfer, my three gorgeous and intelligent daughters were always there when I needed them for encouragement, as well as stuffing and labeling many envelopes. They are always concerned and rally me with the coaching I often give them. Their unconditional love is the essence of ALMERSA Publishing.

Andrew Casey, a gifted psychologist, woke me to the concept that I should do something I like if I want to be happy and successful. He showed me how to avoid self-sabotage, to believe in my abilities, and to take care of my inner child. His concepts provided the basis and inspiration for my Trinity theory.

Diane Sanchez Heiman gave me the opportunity to learn and teach the process of selling. She coached me and gave me the leads to prove myself as an expert salesperson and consultant.

Steve Heiman, the best of the best salespeople, showed me how to prepare for selling, how to sell, and how to sell more. His coaching helped with the really tough customers.

The National Speakers Association (NSA) and the Greater Los Angeles local chapter (GLAC) of the NSA introduced me to many expert authors and speakers. The NSA provided seminars, workshops, and lectures that guided me through the writing and publishing of this book. There is no better group that educates, supports, and nurtures their members.

Thanks goes to Pam Terry at Opus 1 Design for designing my cover and layout, but also for her assistance and recommendations with people and vendors I needed to publish this book. Thanks to Sam Horn for helping me develop the title. Thanks to my editor Ron Kenner at RK Edit. Thanks to Andrea Formato Marin for proofreading. Thanks to Linda Barnett at JSL Printing for creating my promotional materials.

Finally, Sam and Frances Manfer would have been proud. I'm sad they can't hear my THANK YOU in the flesh, but they are in my spirit. I especially appreciate that they taught me how to dig into my spirit for power, and I thank them for the programming that made me believe I can overcome the obstacles and make what I want happen. As they often said, "Things don't happen, you have to make them happen. Pick-up your cross and carry it. You will do great things."

Section I

Up Close
and
Professional

CHAPTER 1

Leaders Make Decisions
Subordinates Do the Legwork

Relationships – we all want them, but how do we get them? Relationships – we all want them, but what do we do with them?

Well, with executive relationships we make money with them – directly or indirectly. We use them to make first sales and follow-on sales. We use them to up-sell. We use them to make peripheral sales. We use them to get information or to gain introductions to other executives. We use them to obtain referrals to executives in other companies. We use them to achieve recommendations. We use them to become positively positioned against competition. We use them so as to be asked to prepare specs for future work. We use them to receive exposure to other executives and subordinates in the organization. We use them to move with the executive as s/he moves up or on to another company.

There are more reasons, but this should be enough to get you motivated. If not, let's look at it from another angle. What happens if you fail to develop relationships with executives? You sell at the lower levels – to purchasing agents, engineers, administrators, supervisors, and functional people. These people need to be sold, but what's the best they can do for you? Recommend — that's all they can do. Selling at the lower levels is tough. You're left in the wings hoping some subordinate will deliver your message accurately and effectively. That's a big hope and a bigger risk. Besides, subordinates usually tell the decision-making executive in charge about why they want something, not why something fits the executive's wants.

If you're selling at the lower level only and the executive hasn't been part of your selling process, then s/he has probably not connected with this expenditure; and, to avoid risk, says, "No." So the subordinate or agent walks away confused and then passes his misunderstanding down to you. You get nothing but pathetic excuses and slight hopes and recommendations to hold-on and be patient.

This is why you often feel like you're spinning your wheels when you're selling. You don't understand what the executives are thinking — the real reasons. If you're connected, if the executives are part of your selling process, they will tell you the real reasons. These could be good or bad, but at least then you'll know what you have to work with.

Executives are paid to make decisions. If they make good ones they stay or move up the organizational ladder. While making decisions, the executive gathers information, analyzes it, filters it through her or his intelligence/experience mechanisms and decides. From such a perspective, these decisions are good for the company and good for the executive. Think of it this way, there are not many executives who make bad decisions for themselves. Even the really nice salt-of-the-earth corporate team player decides based on what's in it for her/him. S/he may talk about the company or budgets, but bottom line, the decision-making is about him or her. So understanding what's good for the executive, from the executive's perspective, is your key to winning the executive and her decision.

Along the same selfish path, executives don't like to take unnecessary risks. If something is working, why change? If what you are delivering is working and the executive associates you with those positive results, you will have on-going business and keep competitors away. If the executive believes there is sufficient benefit from change to overcome the risk of failure, and if he associates you with the greatest positive benefit to risk ratio, you will win the business.

Thus if you know what the executive fears, you have another key – the one to why the sale has stalled or stopped, or why you lost.

So how do you learn what results, wants and fears are relevant to this executive? You have to ask her or him. Without that, you can go through all the subordinates, agents and administrators with the weak hope that they know and have the ability to influence the executive. This is what many salespeople do and then wonder why they feel powerless. The better approach is to use the subordinates and other influential executives to get to the executive in charge of the decision so that then you can learn first hand and do the influencing yourself.

Once you get there, you can learn her/his benefits and fears and show this executive how s/he can get the benefits without the risk of failure. Without this knowledge of the executive, you are making presentations and phone calls with only the hope of hitting something relevant to this executive – and you're doing it through a subordinate or agent. Lots of risks here, wouldn't you say?

Knowing what's in it for the executive and showing how you can give it to her/him is how you start the relationship. As you succeed in delivering results and benefits, the relationship gets stronger. The credibility starts building and the executive trust you will be able to deliver more and more for her/him. S/he then starts approving the purchase of more and different types of your products/services, and you win.

If you're hung up on the subordinate, the purchasing agent, the brokers or administrator being the decision-maker, consider this. These people can maintain a sale – they can continue to approve buying the same product. If you're the incumbent, keep these people happy. But keep in touch with the executives, too, because your competition is hammering away trying to find an in. The one who appeals to the executives wins. The one who stays locked in only with the agents and subordinates loses.

There are probably two major concerns right now. One, how do I get to the executive? Two, how can I succeed when all the executive wants is a lower price. The quick answers are: one, sell the subordinates and other executives on getting you to the executive in charge of the decision; and two, realize that executives buy for big results, results that personally benefit them while carrying minimum risk. They don't buy on price.

So it all comes down to the decision-making executive. To make the first sale, you need to learn about what's important to the executive, and then show that you can deliver it. To continue selling to this account, you have to continue to learn what's important, and continue to deliver. This is what makes a professional relationship.

CHAPTER 2

The Sale:
A Beginning
An End and
What's In-Between

A sale begins anywhere you get your foot in the door. A sale ends in the executive suite. After that, the information flows down. If you're connected in the executive suite, you get to influence the top decision-maker for this purchase. You get the information first. If you're at the subordinate level, the purchasing or administrative level, you don't get a chance to participate in the decision. You get the information last.

Being connected in the executive suite gives you the unfair advantage. You can avoid bidding, pricing, and competitive issues. Executives don't care about these things. They care about solutions that protect or enhance their career in their company. If you can learn what they value and show them how to get it through you, then you will have the beginnings of a solid executive relationship. This will be the start of your selling advantage. Those who have sold successfully know the advantages of getting to the real executive decision-maker.

If you're stuck at the subordinate level or with purchasing or with administrators, it stinks. These people cannot decide. At best, they can recommend. You suck their wind, do their tasks, and take their abuse. Yet they create or complete nothing without executive approval.

If this sounds strange or crazy, then you've never had a proper education in selling. However, most salespeople have never received a proper education in selling. In actuality they learn by trial and error. In all probability they received a marketing briefing about the products/services, a sales manual, and a push out the door. They may have gotten some one day to two week sales training, which was lost after the first two days after the session. However the party was remembered.

But you're saying, "I can't get to these executives. There are gatekeepers and they will get really upset if I go around them. Besides, these gatekeepers will make the decision." "Even if I wanted to get to these executives they are busy and don't want to see salespeople... and... and..."

You're right to all those buts (except about the gatekeeper, subordinate, etc., making decisions). I didn't say it was easy. Nothing worthwhile, like an unfair selling advantage, ever is. However, there is a process that will help you gain access to these executives. There is a process to talk and communicate with them so that they want to spend their valuable time with you. There is a process to develop and to maintain positive, professional relationships with these executives. There is a process of leveraging these relationships to avoid bidding, pricing, budgeting, and competitive issues. Believe it or not these processes will make selling easier and your revenue coffer fuller. This is the beginning.

So if you're interested in learning about these processes, read on. If you're interested in making your selling life easier and more productive, do the exercises. Make the concepts fit your style because at the end of the day you're the one who has to own it and run with it.

CHAPTER 3

Marketing, Selling, and Executive Relationships
What You Didn't Learn in College

Selling is usually confused with marketing. However, the key to selling is establishing executive relationships. Confusing, isn't it? However, this is to be expected since almost no one ever got an education in selling.

Salespeople feel that when they are out promoting, presenting, and exposing people to their company and products/services, they are selling. What they are really doing is marketing, advertising. Salespeople tend to advertise a great deal because they have been conditioned that way by the marketing departments and from what they've observed of other salespeople.

The most successful salespeople work on establishing executive relationships rather than on advertising. They know executives make the decisions and establishing executive relationships is the most powerful tool for closing first and then for follow-up sales. So let's discuss the difference and show how they relate to selling.

Marketing

Marketing is a highly popular discipline. Huge sums of money are spent on marketing. People earn college degrees in marketing. I even have an MBA with a focus in marketing.

Marketing is an exposure, enticement, image building and numbers function. The purpose is to make the masses or target groups aware of your types of products/services and then get them to come to you. *Expose* people to options they didn't know existed and *entice* them to change from what they now use or do. Marketing is building your company and brand image. Marketing creates a favorable impression of your company so that when you approach prospects they will be open to you.

Advertising is a big part of marketing. It is a broad-brush approach focused on the masses of your target market. Advertising is about showing and telling people that, among competitors, your products are the best.

Marketing, selling and executive relations are related. However, marketing dominates the education process in an organization. Who runs advertising? – The Marketing Dept. Where do you get product training? – The Marketing Dept. Where do you learn about your target market and customers? – The Marketing Dept. Marketing explains what we should look for and what we should present.

So salespeople get a marketing approach to selling and become a marketing extension. They go out advertising. They develop better commercials. They make every effort to give a presentation. They take presentation courses. Salespeople leave product training with the impression that if they present a 30-minute commercial about their company and products to enough people, they will achieve sales. Even if our success rate is low, one thinks, we'll get more sales if we call on more people. Salespeople and managers subconsciously and consciously get sucked into this. They feel their role is to knock on every door in their target market and convince every soul to buy their products/services. This is marketing, not selling.

Selling

Whether you are a salesperson, sales manager, CEO or business owner, your biggest responsibility is to bring in sales. Without sales you have no business. So selling is the end point, the bottom line.

Selling is: (1) Finding people who want to change to products/services such as you have, (2) Fitting your product/service to this change in a way that appeals to them more than your competition, and (3) Winning the votes of the powerful, highly influential people – the senior executives.

Since very few people ever formally learned how to sell, then how did we learn to sell? We watched and listened, particularly to marketing input. The more we do what we think marketing is saying, market/advertise, the more we are rejected as pushy and overbearing. Then one day we realize, I am this Willie Loman rejected salesperson. But successful salespeople don't feel that way. They are proud, confident professionals, not to mention being among the best paid individuals in their companies.

Executive Relationships

Establishing executive relationships is the key to selling. With executive relationships, powerful people in the decision making process give you critical information and get you introduced to other powerful, influential people so that you can qualify that there is a deal and then affect the buying decision in your favor.

Look at the most successful salespeople in your organization. They connect with the executives in their accounts. They nurture those relationships. They use those relationships to obtain information and introductions to more prospects. They know when to market. More importantly, they are always trying to position themselves in front of other executives. Look at your own sales. You've probably had more success when you have been connected with senior executives.

Executive relationships require 'winning over' the executives. To win executives over you have to know what is important to each executive and show each one that you can deliver this to him/her. To learn this you need to interview each and so you need introductions. If you have at least one good relationship, you can use that to gain an introduction to the other executives.

In selling you have to position yourself and your company favorably with these decision-makers against competition. To do this you need access to critical information about the decision-makers, about their perception of the competition, their decision process, the sense of urgency, the funding, etc. You need to develop a strategy to address these issues and win. Again, if you have relationships with these senior executives you can ask for the critical information and necessary introductions. You will then be able to develop effective action plans to win. This is the information/introduction highway and the world of executive relationships.

Many salespeople believe that to develop executive relationships they have to be up-close and personal with an executive. The salesperson feels s/he must spend a great deal of social time treating the executive to high impact entertainment. This is simply not true.

Executive relations are about helping executives do their jobs better so that they can preserve or enhance their careers. Executives work because they need a job, a job that helps them meet their personal desires. These desires could be money that affords a style of living, power that feeds one's ego, a challenge that feeds the intellect, a sense of contribution that feeds one's social needs, etc. That's why these people work. Think of Bill Gates, George W. Bush, school principals, and spiritual leaders. Why do they work? Think of yourself, your boss, the CEO of your company. More than anything, except for the health of their families, executives want their work problems solved. Their work lets them retain, attain, or maintain their personal desires.

If you are associated with helping an executive solve pressing problems that positively affect her or his present and future career positions, s/he will want to have a relationship with you. You are a resource to this person. She or he wins because you can help, and you win because this individual will help you improve your position in her or his company. This is Win/Win and the basis of establishing executive relationships. It is also the basis for selling.

Tying Marketing, Selling and Executive Relationships Together

Selling is about developing leads and/or qualifying people who want to change. Qualified leads are people who want to change and thus you must have an offering that enables that change. If you call either by phone or in person and ask a functional person if he wants to change and he says 'no' to change, you have a problem. But you're there so you might as well do some **marketing** to expose and entice. If the person still says he doesn't want to change, you have to move on – either to another person or to another company/division. Many salespeople feel that when the prospective customer doesn't want to change, their job is to convince this person to change. Convincing is not marketing or selling. And it's not your job. Finding qualified leads is. So move on when there is no interest.

If the person you contacted shows an interest in changing, with or without your marketing efforts, you now must **sell**. Qualify to be sure they are right for your product/service and your company. Next, position yourself by 'differentiating' to be selected as the supplier to this person. Then, use this person to move higher up in the organization to reach the powerful and high influence people to see if they, too, want to change. If not, market to entice. If no luck – move on. However, if 'yes,' now you must get these executives to vote for you. And to do this, you need to **establish relationships**.

If you are the incumbent, you want those executives to continue voting for you while your competition keeps trying to penetrate. You must continue to **market** – expose and entice to new concepts, technologies, and applications. You must continue to *sell* — probe to see if they are considering changing. Change is OK. You want to be the pro-active one providing solutions as to how you can continue to solve their changing needs and problems. This is how you will continue the *executive relationship*. Unless they want to change from your company, don't get nervous about change. If they want to change from your company, then re-establish your relationships – if it's not too late.

As you can see, these are closely related yet very different disciplines. If you are marketing to a senior executive, you'll have a tough time getting to him and you'll never develop credibility, because you are advertising. Think how much you enjoy advertising when you're watching TV. Instead of marketing your stuff, probe for areas of interest, changing conditions, or unsatisfied expectations. This will provide the scent of an opportunity and move you towards establishing a *relationship*.

If you're selling (showing your fit and doing proposals) and the person isn't buying or changing – you're wasting your time. You should be marketing — exposing and enticing to see if he or she is open to change. Otherwise, move on.

If you're trying to close a deal by selling and the senior executives don't know you or your company, you're no better than the competition and they will decide on the lowest price. You should be establishing executive relationships.

As you can see there is a place for all three, and you could develop a bunch of combinations. Know when to use each.

CHAPTER 4

Professional Relationships
Social Relationships

Relationships

A relationship will be established when each party feels the benefit for oneself. Executives are primarily interested in business benefits you can deliver that serve them. Business benefits are in your control. Social relationships may or may not follow and may not be in your control. Relationships are dynamic conditions and expectations are continuously changing, but both parties need to keep winning with the other.

Professional Relationships

In business, professional relationships are the strongest relationships because each party contributes to the other's job performance. Job performance is the most important concern for an executive and probably for you. Job performance gives business people the opportunity to get what they really want – money, family security, recognition, kudos, and maybe a promotion. Improving productivity, increasing sales, reducing costs are not the executives' end goals. These are what they are paid to provide to the company. If he does it well, he has the opportunity to get what he really wants.

As a vendor you can help an executive do his job better, but you can't help him get what he really wants. You can only help with what he's paid to do. An executive can help you do your job better (more profitable sales), but cannot give you what you really want. He can only help with the opportunity. Bosses or others in your respective companies or industries can give you what you really want.

So in a professional relationship you can only indirectly influence the benefit each wants for him/herself. Yet the professional relationship is the strongest because the want is so important that any thing you do to help get it is very powerful. Conversely, any perception to adversely affect the path to attainment will be loaded with debilitating fear and resistance.

Social Relationships

Social relationships are different because you can give the other person directly what s/he wants. If a person is looking for a friend or a permanent partner, you can do that. Unfortunately, executives are not looking for friends or partners. They are looking to keep their job, protect their income, get promoted, gain recognition, etc. You can't give them that. You can only provide little things, which are nice, but not significant enough to weather competition, economic downturns, or poor job performance. This is why ball games, dinners, and high impact entertainment doesn't solidify deals or cement your position.

Professional and social relationships become confused in selling. Salespeople and sales managers try to become buddies with executives or subordinates in order to improve their chances of success. Other than friendly initial conversation, there is no need for interaction outside the office. Actually executives feel as though they are doing you the favor of letting you take them to lunch or golfing or out to dinner. Entertainment is not why he wants you. S/he can socialize without you and with the people s/he loves to be with. Even if you become one of his best friends and something goes wrong with what you are suppose to deliver to him professionally, he will drop you professionally. You'll hear something like this, "Don't take this personally, it's business." I don't care if you're the GodFather to his children. It's his career or you. You do the math.

This is why social relationships in business are weak. Besides, in client-vendor relationships there is always the shadow of impropriety. There is an undertone that exists cautioning the client not to let loose, and warning the vendor to hold back from pushing. The concern is the job. Others could perceive the relationship the wrong way and this could jeopardize the job or career.

Treat social events as a 'thank you' for doing business with you. They are nothing more than that. I don't even recommend them as an icebreaker or a get to know you tactic. Many that read this will argue that social relationships and entertainment is what got them in the door and what keeps them there. I'd argue that this is not a good relationship because the bond is only as strong as the entertainment. If your competition offers more, you're out. Where does it stop?

What really happens in social events is that the client gets to know you and starts developing a sense of trust in you. Trust is the secret. Trust that you can deliver what this executive needs to win. If he doesn't trust you, he won't buy. Even if he doesn't like you — but trusts you — he could still buy.

Therefore getting the executive to trust you should be your mission and there are more effective ways to accomplish this than socializing. Show him you can deliver what he wants? Prove you can deliver what he wants? Stop and think about how to do this. The answers will get you on your way to a solid professional relationship. This is your challenge. If the executive feels you can deliver what will help him professionally, he will be all over you.

As a final note, the people most impressed with social events are the subordinates and the salesperson. Salespeople love to brag about all the events they take customers to. Customers rarely talk about it. Actually, they like to keep such things quiet. Once again, do the math. Customers, especially executives, are more interested in their job and their careers. This is what they love to talk about and job talk is usually inappropriate for social events. Go figure.

Reasons We Don't Form Relationships

The purpose of this section is to get you to admit to the reasons that you don't develop relationships with particular executives. If you can do this, then, if you choose, you can develop a strategy to put into effect. Executives are different for each sale and executives are different from each other. So there are going to be different reasons why you don't form relationships with particular executives.

1. I can't get to the executive. Many obstacles stand in the way – people, competitors, subordinates, agents, administrators. The executive doesn't answer his phone. He doesn't return my phone calls. I can't get an appointment and he doesn't see me when I show up.

2. The executive is very busy. He is not interested in what I'm selling. He has people to do this work for him. Besides, this executive doesn't like talking to salespeople.

3. The executive already has a good relationship with a competitor.

4. I don't see any need to see the executive. The subordinate will make the decision or the subordinate will take the message to the executive. Besides if I go past the lower levels, they will get angry and kill any chances for future business.

5. I really don't feel comfortable trying to get to the executive. He's intimidating and I'm uncomfortable talking to him when or if I do get there.

6. I don't know who is the executive in charge of the decision nor do I know any of the other executives. Besides,

once again, even if I knew, how would I get there? The person I'm talking with will feel I just want to get around him.

All of these reasons are very real and very common. This is not just about you. These reasons have substance. People in buying positions have developed approaches that reinforce all of the above and for good reasons. To get the edge over competition, or to determine whether this sale will ever happen, you will have to learn how to slay the dragons, cross the caverns, solve the riddles, and wrestle your own demons. Actually it's a lot simpler than that, if you know how. Do the following workshop and then read on.

Workshop

Consider a situation and the executives involved and select the reason that fits from the list above. Make a note of this and we'll use it later.

Don't get defensive or make any excuses. I'm not asking you to do anything but see if one of these fits. If none of the above fit, email, write, or call me with the reason that does fit so I can include it in my next printing.

Section II

Overcoming the Obstacles Getting to Executives

In order to develop a positive relationship with an executive decision-maker you must personally meet that executive. This may sound obvious, but if you've never met someone, yet you're selling into the account, you may feel you have a relationship. This is not true. Even if s/he knows your name and says hello, it doesn't mean you have a relationship. We'll pursue this further but for now, believe me, you have to meet the executive to have a relationship.

There are seven major reasons why this may be tough:

1. You don't know who it is.
2. Gatekeepers and others block you.
3. You're uncomfortable or intimidated.
4. The executive has no reason to see you, and besides s/he is busy.
5. You feel it's unnecessary to meet the executive.
6. You're at the wrong level to meet this executive.
7. There is an embedded competitor.

My goal is to work through the above reasons and give you the tools to get to the executives.

CHAPTER 5

Obstacle 1
Identifying the
Powerful Executives

Executives

The first step is to know who the executives are. Executives are people in charge of functions and responsibilities. For those of you not use to getting to executives, knowing who the right executives are is a problem. So let's define who they are.

> Any senior manager who has *direct responsibility* for an area, department, or process in the company that your product/service **touches** and/or any senior manager who is **significantly impacted** by your products and services is an executive you should try to get to know.

This definition is a matrix approach rather than a vertical decision-making hierarchy. Many departments and people are affected by the decisions of only one department. Therefore, the feedback and approval from others in the organization are

CORPORATE ORGANIZATION CHART

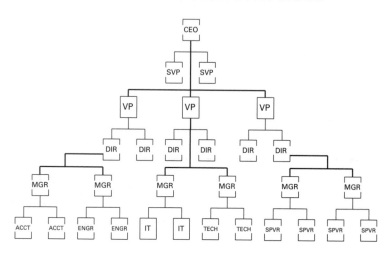

seriously considered. These other departments are areas of **hidden buyers**. You can't cover everyone who could be affected, but you must be conscious of the departments' executives who all these impacted people report to.

For example, I sell consulting services focused on selling that directly touch Sales Management, but my thinking goes to, "Who else is involved with sales and/or touches the customer?" This opens my vision to marketing, customer service, application engineering, proposal people, financial, legal, operations and the CEO. The selling process affects all of these departments. If the VP-Operations makes some disparaging remarks about investing in sales consulting to the VP Sales or blurts out something in a staff meeting, this will have an adverse effect on my success. Therefore, it's in my best interest to have a conversation with the VP-Operations.

When I'm selling solutions and processes to improve sales productivity, etc., I'm focusing mostly on sales and marketing executives, but my desire is to get higher to the CEO or General Manger. Sales volume, customers, and competition significantly affect these people. However, I am also conscious that other executives in tangential departments are affected and will influence the decision. These are the hidden buyers who can kill my sale without me having a clue. The Field Service Manager, the Engineering Manager, the Financial Manger, etc., are all people I need to consider. These executives will have to work with their people to build positive customer relationships in their domains and bring back valuable information to my customer's salespeople. They will be part of the selling process and could impact my sale.

If you're selling software and your focus is IT, you must consider the executives in charge of those tangential departments. What people are touched and/or are impacted by your product/services and who are the senior managers of those people?

Executives have power beyond their own domain. They are the management team and they participate in corporate decisions. They influence decisions and other executives. They are the corporate leaders and advise each other for their own good and for the good of the company.

Non-Executives

Managers and senior managers are responsible for functions. Supervisors are responsible for people's activities – scheduling, productivity, and behaviors. Supervisors have power only in their own departments. They can influence decisions and their degree of influence is based on their credibility with executives. Supervisors never make ultimate decisions that involve change – unless it is an "or equal" brand change. Supervisors never have financial responsibility other than staying within their budgets. They can't even spend their budget without getting approval from their boss, the executive.

Finally, purchasing agents are not executives. They may wear ties and have an office, but once again they cannot approve a decision to change. They must obtain approval from a functional leader. Not even the VP Purchasing can approve it unless it directly involves the purchasing department. VPs or directors of purchasing have power, but not on functional aspects. They control the administration of terms and conditions of the purchase agreement, and procuring parts and supplies that meet the technical specifications. Functional people established all of these.

Now supervisors, purchasing people, and a host of other administrators can veto or keep you out by saying you don't fit some specification or condition or that they are just not interested. Therefore, you can't ignore or blow-off these people. However, only a senior executive can say 'yes' and make it happen. One of these executives has the power and the other executives significantly influence the power. Get to know the power and these other executives and stop limiting yourself to the non-executives. How you do this will be discussed as we move ahead.

Doing the Digging

You've identified some of the departments and functional people in the organization that your product/service touches, so who are the executives who run these departments? The best way to find out is to ask people. This involves networking. You can also search public information such as annual reports, 10Ks, company web sites for executives. This is a good source of hierarchical information, but be careful. It doesn't list who the ultimate decision-maker for your products/services is. It does list, however, the functional executives, at very high levels. If it's a billion-dollar plus corporation these may be too high for you to get started, but it's good to know who they are. It depends on what you're selling. Public sources may be dated, although web sites are usually current. So now you have to start digging.

The Getting Started Technique – Sleep on it.

Digging can be fun and productive, or difficult, time consuming and laborious work. Let's make it productive and as much fun as possible. Your attitude is the key. Keep it upbeat and challenging. We all love a good challenge. We love games. We love to win. Some may not like others to lose, but we all love to win. What turns a challenge into a misery is our mental state. So start the digging when you are mentally ready for this, but you must prepare. I prefer the first thing in the morning. I'm fresh and have not been worn down by all the issues of the day. However, I have mentally prepared for it the night before by making it an agenda item for the next day.

This mental preparation is critical. It gets you thinking about what you're going to do and gives you a means to stay on track. The technique, as you will see, is used throughout this book in different ways and will be a very powerful tool for you.

When I was starting to write this book, I was undergoing a number of personal problems. Three big sources of income had evaporated because I didn't maintain good executive relationships. The people I partnered with in my consulting business retired and sold their interest to people who had a different vision of what our business should be. My three daughters were in college, just leaving college with no job, or just going into college. I had major cash problems. My thoughts were focused on the sadness of losing some business, the hurt, sadness, and anger of losing my partners, and the fear of making enough money to pay all my expenses. However, each night before I went to bed, or during the night when my mind started its tormented cycle, I'd say to myself, "I've got to write my book. That is my morning focus. No matter what, I will give it two hours."

Now identifying executives is not as challenging as writing a book, but what's similar is that both are problems. We need a process to get ourselves mentally prepared, and the best time is before leaving the office or after your last call. Your last business task of the day is to prepare a to-do list for the next day. On this list, include digging for an executive. Put it on paper. Then sleep on it. The creative ideas and the eventual results will astound you.

I learned this technique early in life. I attended a Catholic elementary school and we would sing hymns at Sunday Mass. A tough, no nonsense nun was in charge of teaching, rehearsing and coordinating this effort. Early in the week she'd come into our class and start teaching us this hymn which was totally unfamiliar and boring. We were awful. However, she stuck with it for a half-hour. Her parting words whenever she left were, "Sleep on it." The next day when we did it again, it was great. I was always amazed.

The process is fairly simple. You establish a concept – the hymn, or the need to identify an executive decision-maker. Once you establish it, your subconscious kicks in and plays the tune over and over again. It makes it familiar and comfortable. For your executive search, your subconscious generates ideas to move you forward. It will actually produce visions of your doing and accomplishing what you want to accomplish. It makes you feel familiar and comfortable with the idea. So in the morning not only do you have ideas, but you feel confident enough to follow through with them.

You don't even need to do it overnight, but what you do need to do is give some space between saying you want a solution to a problem and getting feedback from yourself. That is, identify what you have to do, or what you need, or what you have to solve, etc. Then **write it down**. I'm a firm believer in writing it down because you get it out of your system and give it reality. This means it's not merely a thought but something that needs attention. Additionally, writing it down keeps you from forgetting about it as other stuff crosses your mental monitor. It keeps flashing at you once you have a chance to catch your breath.

After you write it down, go do something else. Get a cup of coffee, take a break, make a call to a customer, visit someone, do another task, go to bed, whatever. You have to give it some space. This could be five minutes to a day. When you come back, read what you wrote and start writing ideas. Just let them flow whether or not they make sense. Get them all out of your mind and then select the ideas or actions you feel most comfortable doing.

See your mind is a factory. Give it the orders and it will produce what you've requested. I'll explain how this works later. Meanwhile, sleep on it.

What Level of Executive to Pursue

The executive in charge of the decision for your products and the executives who influence this executive will change from company to company and from time to time depend on two primary factors. These factors are (1) the impact your product/service has on the company, and (2) the size of the company. Answer these questions. What is the strategic importance of your product service? How much of it is used and/or how often is it used? What alternatives are there? How big a change is there for the company to switch? What is the impact/benefit to the company to change? How big a risk is it for the company? How big are the dollars to purchase compared to other expenditures?

The answers to these questions will determine how high you have to go. Let's look at size vs. product/services impact. See *Matrix 1*. The greater the impact, change, risks or dollar amounts to the company the higher the decision and influence will go. If your product/service has major impact on the company and it's a small company, you will have to focus on getting to the CEO and Sr. VPs. If there's a big impact and a big company, your target will be Sr. VP and VP's. The bigger the impact the higher the level. If it is a small impact and a small company, your targets will be VP and managers. If it is small impact and big company, your targets

Impact of Product/Service vs. Size of Company

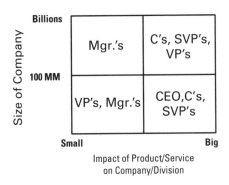

Impact of Product/Service
on Company/Division

Matrix 1

will be director and managers. Therefore a key test is to determine the impact it will have on a company. Big impacts, changes, risks, and dollars usually affect profits, productivity, and sales (ability to sell and deliver more).

Capital expenditures and big dollar purchases also require high level approvals. Another key test is money. If ever the person you are talking with flinches, hesitates, or argues about the money, you are at the wrong level. You have to move up. The person in charge of the decision will never struggle with the money. He will struggle with what he's getting for the money (return) or the risk of the venture relative to the return, but not the absolute dollar amount. This leads to a great qualifying question to determine if you're at the right level. "Is the cost of this investment a problem?" See how he answers this. If there are any words like, "It's very expensive. It's not in the budget. Times are tough," then this person is worried about affording it or getting the money. Anything that sounds like money problems is your indicator that the decision-maker is at a higher level. It may even be beyond the top officer of the company. He may have to go outside to investors or a financial institution.

Consider the following examples.

PRODUCT/SERVICE	IMPACT	EXECUTIVE LEVEL
Health Insurance to any company	Big	CEO, CFO
Jet Engines to Boeing	Big	CEO, CFO, COO
Electrical Wire to Boeing	Small	VPs – Engr, Purchasing, OP's

Comment: Lots used, many alternative suppliers, small relative dollars

Printing for SG Manfer, Sales Consultants	Big	Owner

Comment: Major cost item relative to other expenses

Note: Purchasing will be involved in all of these, but will not make final decisions.

Workshop

Think of an account that you are currently selling to. What departments does your product/service touch or what people does it impact? Who manages these departments or people? Who does this manager report to?

Write the answers down on *Form I-A*. It is critical that you write it down. As you will see, keeping it in your head will not serve you and you won't progress beyond your current position. It's too easy to forget, ignore, rationalize, and avoid. So put it on paper. You're chances of remembering this and of gaining the advantages of your reading effort will increase fourfold.

If you don't know the information, that's OK, but admit to yourself that you don't know. Then you'll at least know you don't know and you might encourage yourself to find out. You will learn how to find out soon.

FORM I
(A) Identifying the Executives

Departments Your Product/Service Impacts or Touches	Direct Impact or Touches	Key Executive of Dept. (Name/Title)	Other Important People in Department (Name/Title)

CHAPTER **6**

Your Network
Using What Resources You Have

Hopefully by now you are getting the point that there is a
key executive and other executives that you need to meet.
However, first you need to identify who they are. This is where
you start to use your network. You have at your disposal a
very powerful network. Through years of experience, through
your company, through your acquaintances, through friends,
etc., you have a wealth of contact information. You have probably never come close to tapping it. The world where you participate is very small. Somebody you know knows somebody
you want to know. You are only a few contacts away from
knowing anyone.

Try this exercise. Think of a company ABC where you'd
like to make a sale. Got it. Now think of a person in a key
functional position where you'd like to start developing a relationship – maybe a VP Information Technology. Most likely

you don't know that person. So stop and think of anybody in your company — acquaintances, vendors of complimentary product/services, consultants, teachers, managers, etc. — who know anything about ABC. Call that person and tell them you want to develop a relationship with the VP of Information Technology of ABC. Ask that person if she would help you get to speak with that person. If she says she doesn't know that person (which will be the most likely answer) ask her if she knows somebody who does or knows somebody who knows somebody. You'll be surprised how effective this is for obtaining the names of the people you want to identify. But you can't stop with the name. You need to talk with this individual even though there is no reason for that person to take up any of his time for you. That is, unless you know something about this person's priority problems that you could help solve, or unless your contact will introduce you.

So when you're asking your network person the name of the next network person, you also need to ask for a means for you to get to talk with this person. For example "And by the way, can I impose on you to call Ms. X and ask if I can talk to her about a solution to the problem you just mentioned to me?" Ask for help and your network person will usually help. Don't be macho or shy. Remember, "God helps those who help themselves." Also, don't forget to email or send a thank you note.

Most salespeople I've worked with are taken back by the dual task of identifying both the executive and the priority issues facing that executive. As salespeople we all feel that the problems our products/services solve should be at the top of our targeted executive's priority list. If it's not, then it becomes our mission to convince the executive it should be high priority. This is the reason you have trouble getting to see these people. They don't want to be convinced. They want help with their own issues.

> Your mission should be to identify both the executives involved and the priority issues facing each person. Then determine if your product/service can

directly help. If it can, you need an introduction from your network person. If it can't, then you will get nowhere with this executive and this will be your first indicator you should move on to another executive and/or another company.

Here is a personal story to demonstrate this point. There is a Senior VP of Sales that I wanted to develop a better relationship with. We had a positive relationship and we communicated by email on an infrequent basis. I knew that to make more sales in this account I would have to be recognized by her as a contributor to her success. I was consulting with her company (thanks to her) and I saw management and training issues that needed correcting. I knew I could help. So I approached her about it. She was very polite. She asked a few quick questions to put it in her frame of reference and then said she'd look into it. I asked her to get back to me, but never heard back from her. Later I heard from other sources she had passed the observations down.

The point here is I did nothing to improve my relationship with her. Matter of fact I probably hurt it. I gave her another thing to worry about that had a secondary priority and did nothing to address her primary priorities. Why should she take the time to get back to me? Call my action stupid and you're right. I was focused on my observations. I didn't take the time to inquire about her priority issues. I didn't do anything to prove I could help her. Therefore there was no reason to get back to me. I guarantee this executive will not go out of her way to see me until I do something to help her with her priority issues.

At this point you're probably saying to yourself, I don't even know who the executive is and now I'm supposed to know this person's personal issues. Well, the answer is 'yes,' you're right. I do want you to know both pieces and you'll find it through your **network**.

The following points are what will make networking successful.

- First, you have to open your mind to the reality that you know people that know people.

- Second, you have to be proactive to do the digging. It is much easier to call the receptionist and ask for an executive's name and extension, but your chances of getting anywhere are slim to none. Don't feel afraid, anxious, ashamed, etc., about calling someone for help. Remember that people like to help other people. Check the Internet and other public sources. These won't give you the up close and personal stuff, but they will give a feel of what the company is all about.

- Third, you have to frame your question so you get the information you're seeking. Don't ask initially, "Do you know anybody at ABC Company?" You may get all sorts of random information. Rather, ask if s/he knows the VP of IT or someone who knows the VP of IT. If the answer is no, then who does s/he know who might be able to network you to the VP of IT for ABC Company?

- Fourth, ask your contact to call that person to set up a conversation for you. Your contact will have credibility of sort with this new contact and you need this introduction to get through voice mail and other screens. You don't want your contact to get the information and relay it to you. If the information is relayed, some will be lost, it will be limited, and probably not in the form that helps you the most. You want to talk to the new contact yourself. Then when you get to this new contact, listen and let the person talk. You will gain valuable insight that can help you move forward.

- Fifth, when you get to someone who knows the VP of IT be sure to ask what issues are facing the VP of IT. Remember not to sell. Make this person part of the process. Start building your relationship with this contact. You never know where it will take you. Again, DON'T SELL. Ask questions and listen to the answers. Ask for suggestions.

- Thank her/him and ask if s/he would like to hear how you would approach the situation with your new wealth of information and if s/he wants to hear what happens. Consider this person was a resource for you and you may need her/him again

Now write down your first contact's name on Form I-B and fill in the other information you know. Write down what you need to know. What are you going to do? Sleep on it.

FORM I
(B) Network

Names of People to Ask For Help?	What Will You Ask Them? – Information/Introduction

CHAPTER **7**

Leveraging,
Building a Golden Network:
The Info/Intro Highway

Your Golden Network is your *information and introduction* highway. It's your path to the executive suite. It consists of people who have benefited from working with you. These people will give you information about the executives and get you introductions to the executives who are involved in the decision making process. If you are already selling to an account, your Golden Network is in place waiting to be used. If you're still trying to make an initial sale to an account, you need to start building your Golden Network.

Existing Accounts
People you've worked with previously will help you because they realize you can help them. You've established credibility with them and they trust you. They've received benefits from your services and want more. They probably even like you as

a person. So they are willing to help because there is something in it for them. What may be different for you is the task of *working* these people to get information and introductions. I stress the word *working* to keep you focused on moving to the executive suite. You can not be complacent with your best contacts. It is too limiting. You are not giving up on these people. They know as well as you that decisions are made by the executives and that it would be good for all of you to be connected. You may not like the word "working," so select something that sounds softer.

Keep in mind that these golden network people are not focused on this, they are not thinking of 21 ways to help you every time they see you. Actually you are probably not even on their radar screen. So *you* have to take the initiative. That's why I say, ask for their help. They want to help. They won't mind. So, work them. Working here is a good thing. You are exercising their knowledge base and filling up yours.

Before I started writing this section today, I was trying to get to a key executive in one of my existing accounts — NCS Learn, a division of Pearson Education. I want more consulting work from them and I know I have to get to the new executives. However, all is not good. With all the changes there are different camps about my sales processes. Therefore, I have to take advantage of the good and clean up the not so good issues. I have to meet these new decision-makers and learn what's on each one's mind.

So I went to my Golden Network. These are people who see the benefit of my services and would like to use more of them because they are not eager to change to something that could be less beneficial and require more training. However they have constraints imposed by the top executives. So what I've done is make sure each one on my Golden Network still feels good about my sale processes. Since they do, I've asked them to help me build a strategy to get me to see and sell upper management. We've discussed what's important to the key executives and have determined the best approach for me to get to the new executives. Now each one is working to get me interviews with each of their bosses. Once there, I will try to convert the bosses and have them get me to the CEO. The important point is to keep asking for information and introductions that will help me convert and sell these executives and the CEO. It sounds simple and it is.

New Accounts

With a new account you have to develop a Golden Network. No buyers have experienced any benefits from your products, yet. So your initial job is to work with your first buyer and help him realize he can get what he wants from your services. If you're successful, you will have to use this person to introduce you to others in the decision making process and the executives. Miller Heiman calls this person a coach. Coaches have to be developed and the way you develop them is to show them that you can provide what they each want. Sound familiar? It should because this is what you do every time you meet a new buyer.

As with making any sale, you have to win the election of the decision-makers, especially those who carry the most votes. These are the influential executives and the power executive for this purchase. In order to get to these influential, well-insulated people, you will have to get your initial buyer to help you meet more people who can eventually get you to the influential executives. This person will want to help because s/he knows that if you win the election, s/he also wins. S/he has made the connection that your services will benefit her/him better than all alternatives. Otherwise s/he will be reluctant to help.

This is why the first sale is so tough. Most buyers are checking out all the options to determine which one will benefit him/her the most. People keep you at arms' length. You have no Golden Network to turn to for help. So you keep bouncing around scratching for information and begging for appointments.

It is important to re-emphasize that both information and introductions are necessary. A story will illustrate.

I was in my office doing some work when I received a call from someone trying to sell me financial planning. He used the name of my close friend as his method to get my attention. So I listened. He told me a little about what he does and what he's done for my friend and others. I basically said I'm not ready and to send me a card – the classic blow-off.

Had this person taken the time to find out from my friend what issues I was facing with my financial future (which are many), he could have used that information to keep my attention and get me involved. He could have also had my friend call me and tell me that this financial planner that he respected was going to call me. He could have also visited my friend's office, which is next to mine. He could have gotten a briefing about me and had my friend introduce him to me with a preface about some issues I'm facing. He had the Golden Network, but he didn't work his contact to give him information or an introduction.

Building Your Golden Network

Many times we make sales without getting involved with any executives. We've worked with purchasing or some of the functional people responsible for spec'ing or using our products/services. Through our proposal and a few meetings/calls to these people, we positioned ourselves to get the order. We may have never talked with the ancillary people or executives. We may have assumed that the purchasing agent, the engineer, the technician, the broker, the consultant, had the power to make the decision.

However, you can be sure there was an executive who approved the decision for our product/service. In addition, this executive probably checked either formally or informally with the other executives whose people touch our product/service.

There are two exceptions. One, your product/service is on an approved list that this lower level purchasing agent, technical person and/or administrator can choose from. Two, your product/service has been used before and this is now a reorder of an approved product/service. Remember, however, someone had to approve you getting on that list initially and/or being used the first time. This executive and the affected executives are whom you want a relationship with. Why? – Because these are the people who will recommend and approve further purchases.

So let's assume you've made a sale without getting close to the executives. Now is the perfect time to get introduced and to start developing a relationship. The executives will want to see you because they want to be reassured that what each expects will be delivered. You should want to meet them to learn what they expect so that you can either deliver it or deal early with the misconceptions.

If you've just made the sale, ask the people you worked with to introduce you to some of the executives or their bosses. If they are resistant, you might say something like, "When we discussed your expectations of my product/service, you said you wanted this, this, this, etc., and I will do everything to make that happen. However, your boss and some other manager who will be affected by my products and services may have a different spin on your expectations. It would be good for both of us to know what each expects from this purchase. Could you arrange for me to meet with some of them?"

This is not bull, either. Thinking of your customer's best interest will make you successful. Those executives want their expectations met and you can't meet them if you don't know what they are. Having your contact tell you his impression of the executives' expectations is risky. You will get your contact's version. This is what he heard; not necessarily what the executives said. – Not because he wants to mislead you. It is human nature. What you hear from each executive may be considerably different.

The executive will appreciate your involvement because you are giving him a chance to be heard on what is specifically important to him – not the party line results. *Party line results* are the expectations of everybody – the generic stuff, i.e., lower cost, productivity, quality, motherhood, and apple pie. They don't reflect what is important to a particular individual – reduce my downtime 20%, eliminate two people from my department. Always remember the party doesn't vote. The individual does. Therefore, if you want that person's vote you must impress the individual.

Once met, keep in touch with these executives during installation to make sure they are aware of progress or delays. 'No surprise' is the rule in business. It is best to hear the news from you. Meet with them again after implementation to discuss successes or issues.

If your product/service has met his expectation, you want to be sure you are associated with delivering solutions and results. Otherwise you will be forgotten. If he is not satisfied, thank him for his candor and tell him you will go back and figure out what to do. You want to be associated as a problem-solver. Otherwise you will be remembered as the problem and you will get no more business.

Now I've only referred to one person, but there were probably a few people who really supported the decision to go with your product/service. Use all of these people as your Golden Network and go through the process discussed above to get to the executives.

If your products and services are already being used, find the people who are enjoying the benefits. These people are your Golden Network. For those people who are not happy with you and/or your goods, use the Golden Network to better understand the dissatisfaction and to get you in front of them. Don't ignore the dark clouds or you'll drown in that account. Let your Golden Network help you.

Workshop

Select an existing account and an executive you would like to meet to develop a relationship with. List your Golden Network of people for that account. Who will introduce you to this executive? What will you ask your Golden Network people about this executive to prepare you for your meeting. Write it down. Sleep on it.

CHAPTER 8

Obstacle 2
Gatekeepers and Blockers

As a salesperson, your toughest assignment when starting in an account is getting to executives. Administrative assistants, receptionists, and subordinate employees protect executives from you. In addition to them, you will block yourself by thinking that people don't want you going around them to get to the executives.

Admins block you because they feel their mission is to keep salespeople away from the boss. You pose a threat to their duties. The quicker they can get rid of you, the faster their fear is relieved. You're a stranger. You're a threat. Besides, you are extra work for them. They have to explain you to the boss and they have to schedule you. It is easier to say "No – not interested." There is no risk.

Receptionists block you because they have been read the rules not to give out information. Besides, they have calls coming through and they don't have time to play 20 questions with you. However, if you have a name they will pass you through. If you don't, they'll either not allow you to go further or pass you to an admin. Receptionists may know a little about the company, such as the names and titles of some people, but they don't know what these people's responsibilities are and how they fit with your offering. I question why you even start with them. Go to an admin of a senior executive.

Now if you get past the receptionist and the admin, you will probably have to deal with voice mail. Most executives are in meetings or traveling and not around to pick up the phone. Actually they will answer if they are in their office, unless the admin is set to intercept. It is more interesting to talk to someone new than face what's on their desk. Some companies even have caller ID and the Exec decides to answer or pass it to voice mail.

Another line of defense is the subordinates and lower level buyers. These could be administrative people who called you in, e.g., purchasing agents. They could be functional people who you know will be involved and you either called them or they called you. It could also be people you were passed off to. These subordinate types are not going to let you through to the exec's office without effort. Besides, they need to be sold.

Finally the most debilitating blocker is you. You feel that the person or people you are talking with don't want you to go beyond them, so you stop yourself. Successful salespeople never think that way. They approach the situation with the confidence that the executives want to see them and knowing that these subordinates will help them get there. Successful salespeople feel that until the subordinate says, in no uncertain terms, "You are not allowed to approach the executives," the objective is the executives.

So it's tough dealing with blockers. However, if we know why we're being blocked we can develop strategies, tactics, and techniques to get through them.

Reason for the Blocks

People block you because *they have nothing to gain* by letting you pass; more importantly, they *stand to lose* by letting you pass.

Admins could be afraid their boss will be irritated, or they feel that if I were my boss I'd be irritated. Who knows what's going on with each admin, but suffice it to say that they sense a loss with no potential for a gain. After a go around with an admin or receptionist, I catch myself saying, "Why is she so tight with information such as the boss' name or email address? Is she afraid I'll send a letter bomb?" When I become rational, I realize that she *is* afraid of a bomb – something that could hurt her in her job or with her boss. Why should she help me? What's in it for her? If her boss finds out, she could get reprimanded – maybe even lose her job. Even if it is not that significant, it's easier to say no and give nothing than to work with you. Again, working with you is an effort and effort is a loss unless there is a reward for her. The same applies to the receptionist. Why extend myself – for what?

Subordinates to the execs are basically the same; however, their loss may take a different spin. They could be afraid of losing control. They could be afraid of losing the allusion that they are the final decision-maker – the Power. They may feel they have been given the task to investigate and decide and if you get by them, they have done a poor job with their task. They may also be afraid that their bosses will get angry if you get past them. They may feel it is their job to deal with you. Whether it is true or not, it is their fear and it is real to them. If you get through, they lose.

It may be that the subordinates are not interested in what you have to offer, so why should they let you go further? It may be they don't want what you have to offer because they don't like change or they don't like your solution. They believe that if you get through to the bosses you could sway them and this will not be good. They may also like your competitor and want to stop you from making any in-roads with them or their bosses. No matter how good you think it will be for them or their company, it is their perception of the loss that is blocking you.

Self-imposed blocks are another matter, but similar. Here you feel you will lose if you go around, so you block yourself. You have to take a different approach to selling. Your objective is to get to and work with all the decision-makers, including the executives. Tell everybody along the way that this is your mission and you want these subordinates to help you get to the executives. This is about confidence and purpose. We'll discuss this later.

The voice mail blocks or screens are also all about losses or gains. Voice mail is really a great way to get to someone. However, it only works well if that person is interested in what you have to say or in who you are. Think about yourself. Your significant other or a good friend calls and leaves you a voice mail. You will listen intently and probably call back as soon as you can. A telemarketer calls, you probably skip or fast forward. But if the telemarketer hits a nerve right away, then you might listen and may even call back. Even if you know the person, or the person calling refers to someone you know, they may capture your attention yet the message will have to hit something sensitive before you'll call back. Bottom line, you will call back if you see something in it for yourself to make it worth calling back – otherwise it is a loss to make the effort to call back or even talk to a telemarketer. So with voice mail, if you want a call back you'll have to know what's in it for the person (gain or loss avoidance).

Now another big reason you can't get through these blockers is because you don't have credibility with them. In other words, they don't trust you to take care of them or keep them safe. However, this too, is about gains and losses. Can they trust you to do something that will be good for them or are they afraid you will do something that will cause them to lose? For example, I could use some help with investments, but I'll never talk with a 'cold call' stockbroker. S/he could be great, but there is no trust and there is a risk of losing my money.

Admins, receptionists, and subordinates block us because we have no credibility with them. If you had some positive history with any of these people, they would do a lot to help you (Golden Network). If they don't know you, they immediately default to, "I can't trust you. Therefore, I can't let you through and I'd like to get rid of you."

Actions to Overcome Blocks

Since the main reason people block you is fear of a loss and/or that there's nothing in it for themselves, your best action is to show them how they will win or at least not lose with you. For example, if an admin knows and trusts you she'll tell you anything, including the gossip. So your strategy is to develop credibility with her by getting her to feel comfortable with you so she feels she will lose nothing. The more secure this individual is the farther you will go. High level admins feel very secure about their position and the people below their boss. They will give you information about lower level people because they have nothing to lose. Getting info about their bosses is another story.

The same is true with subordinates. If they trust you they will be the first to let you get in front of their bosses, because they know they won't lose with you and that you will help them get what they want – your offering.

If they feel they will lose control, for example, you'll have to show them how they will maintain control of the decision and how it is good for both of you to see the executive. You might say, "It would probably be good for both of us if I knew your boss' expectations of my products/services. This way I could structure a proposal that would make both of us look good. So why don't you set a meeting and you can run it. I'll be there for support if you need me. But more importantly, I can hear it directly and we won't miss something and disappoint your boss. This could make both of us look badly."

I was working with CNA, a very large insurance company. I knew I'd never get the consulting deal I was working until I met with the Sr. V. P., and the SalesTraining VP was blocking me. However, in an earlier interview I found out that the Training VP was concerned about his credibility. He had spent many years building credibility with the managers of the sales department and he did not want anything to jeopardize it. Establishing the credibility of training managers is very difficult because they are perceived as not out on the front line. Training is more theoretical than practical, so why listen? Well, this VP had earned his credibility and he was not going to recommend something that could fail and jeopardize losing his credibility.

Knowing this, I talked with the sales managers whom I had already met with and developed a relationship (Golden Network). I explained the problem and they agreed to conference call the VP Training and tell him that they liked my services and wanted to pursue it further. Well this eliminated the credibility issue for the VP Training and he quickly got me in front of the Sr. VP. I got the assignment and this VP Training helped me to get more deals. He learned that I delivered for him. He continued to build his credibility (win) and he continued to help me.

Had I not known his loss issue, I would have done all sorts of things to circumvent him or to please him (such as lower the costs). These would have accomplished nothing and could have cost me time and money. Knowing the loss helped me build the strategy to make it a win for him.

Turning a loss into a win is the best way to approach a block. Have an open, up front conversation with the blocker to find out what s/he is afraid of losing, or what s/he would like to gain by working with you. You can also get help from your Golden Network. Have these people get you information or get you a meeting with the blocker. Be careful, however, about getting loss information from other people. Losses are personal and others usually don't know the personal details.

Another strategy is to go around the blocker. We've all done our share of this. Calling early or late is a way to go around the admin. This and many other techniques are out there for you to find and try, but the problem is that you could get people annoyed or upset with you. It could be the blocker, the executive, or your own company. It depends on the ramifications. So be careful with this strategy.

Another strategy is to go along with the blocker. Sometimes people block you for your best interest. Just keep the dialogue going. Be sure it is in your best interest and not for other reasons. Set a plan with dates and work it together.

CHAPTER 9

Obstacle 3
Executive Intimidation

Feeling uncomfortable, uneasy, and intimidated are the biggest problems preventing people from establishing relationships with key executives. It is understandable and expected because most of your life other people were showing you their fear in dealing with the higher ups. Consequently you developed a fear, an anxiety, an uneasiness, an uncomfortable feeling when faced with the actuality of getting to these people and developing a relationship. Some of the things I listened to while I was growing up were:

"He's a big shot."

"He owns that business and is very powerful in the community."

"She's a very important executive and doesn't spend time with low-level people."

Besides, these people have big offices. They are surrounded with admins and subordinates. They have high level, big, responsible positions. These and other awe-inspiring statements and symbols implant a notion of 'Holier than Thou' – or – 'I'm not worthy.' These messages set up triggers – doubts of self worth – that send a tingle of uneasiness whenever someone tells you to get to this senior level executive. It also triggers uneasiness when you say to yourself, "I know I have to get higher in the organization." Just look at the words – 'higher level.' Does higher imply that I must be lower? Is that higher than the person I'm currently talking to, who is making me feel uncomfortable already? Now I have to get higher yet?

Anxious, uneasiness, uncomfortable, anxiety – it's all about fear: a feeling. This feeling of fear is all about **projection**. You start thinking about getting to this executive and it starts. Maybe you mentally see this busy, bullish, executive in his spacious, well decorated office, and surrounded by admins and subordinates. Maybe you think that this executive has the power to say 'yes' or 'no' to your offering and to you. Since you've been conditioned from childhood to fear authority figures, all you have to do is think of the word 'executive' and you feel uneasy.

Fear happens to you by projecting the future in a negative way. Something bad will happen, so I don't want to go there. We don't even go through the thought processes to fear because we are so conditioned. Unconscious or conscious projection is greatly debilitating. It paralyzes us into a state of shock. We do nothing. We have instilled fear within ourselves.

Fear, uneasiness … is self-induced. You have created the scene and you don't like it. You know what will happen when you try to make contact. You'll get blocked or you'll get rejected and you've got experiences to support that prediction. Therefore you develop rationalizations why you can't get to the executive. You then start strategizing about overcoming these projected problems rather than dealing with the real problem – you.

What make matters worse is that fear is self-fulfilling. You create the disaster that you fear. Since you have this vision of the future based upon old memories or conditioning, you unconsciously prepare yourself for failure. You approach the situation with a timid, fearful, or uneasy attitude that's exuded to the admin, subordinate, or the executive himself. They pick up on this and immediately turn off to you. You get rejected and this reinforces your previous vision. You have created your own demise. This is why negative projection is so devastating and it is so unnecessary.

I coach many salespeople and am amazed at the effort put into reasons one can't get to an executive. After a while, with lots of feedback from associates, they realize it is about them not the executive. Once you admit, "I feel uncomfortable," you can then develop a plan to help you feel comfortable enough to pursue the executive.

Actions to Overcome Uncomfortable and Intimidated

The first thing to do, as noted, is to admit that you feel uneasy. Once you do this, ask yourself why you feel this way. What do you fear? Keep asking until you find an answer. The answer will be that you are projecting a negative outcome; so to overcome this, acknowledge that you don't know what the future will bring. If you have to project, project positively. "Reception to you and or your message will go great." "This person will want to introduce me to his boss so that his boss' expectations are met." If you set your projections towards getting nowhere, chances are you'll get there. You'll exude shyness, uneasiness, hostility or whatever your defense mechanism and you will come across in a negative way. Notice some of the words you've used in the past. "Is it possible for me to speak to so and so?" "Sorry to bother you, but could I ...?" "If you have the time, ..." These are not strong positive statements, so people will blow you off without thinking. Say instead, "Hi, my name is Sam Manfer and I work with companies such as yours creating sales and improving the productivity of sales teams. Would you (not could you) answer two or a few questions?" You could also say, after you introduce yourself, "John, realizing your time is very precious, as is all of ours, would you answer a few questions with me now or should I call later?" If he says later, then ask him when the best time would be. Before you make any call, project in your mind that the person will be happy and open to talk with you. Project positive and positive outcomes will start happening. Even if things don't work out, you will be able to say it was their issue, not yours.

Another action is to develop confidence. We will discuss this further in the book. However, the best way to get confidence is to prepare. Get information about the executive and the company. Talk with people who know the executive and the company. Use your Golden Network. Talk with people in your company and urge them to help you prepare for the sales call or for an effective approach to get an appointment. Remember it is OK to ask for help. People will help gladly, if asked. The more you prepare, the more confident you will feel.

Another action is to realize that this person is human just like you. You both have jobs to do. You both value your time and don't want to waste it. Neither of you wants to be sold. You both want resources to help you with problems. You both get up and get dressed and go to work each day. If you were to see this person on the weekend at a kid's event or at a restaurant, you'd talk to him like you'd talk to any other parent or adult. So get over the 'better than you' syndrome.

CHAPTER 10

Obstacle 4
You Feel the Executive Has No Time or Reason to See You

You may truly believe this or you may be rationalizing. Whatever your reason, the executive needs to get information about your offering. Why? because he is the ultimate authority to approve the purchase of your product/service. Also, the responsibility for what it will accomplish is his. The company needs this and it's his job to get it. Therefore, he needs to know how it will be purchased and implemented and when he'll start receiving the benefits. Somebody has to bring him that information. It can be an internal person or it can be you. He may not care. All he wants is to feel comfortable that it will go right with the greatest chance for success and the least probability of failure. He wants to know what to do if there are problems. Remember, if this goes south – he takes the hit.

If it is a tangential executive, is he significantly impacted or touched? If so, he will also want to know how the product/service will be implemented and how it will help or hurt him or his subordinates. He's going to get the information and you are the best person to give him the information. Therefore, the executive has a compelling reason to see you.

Even so, executives may have other priorities that are pressing when you attempt to talk with them. Don't take this as rejection. This is life. Use your Golden Network to keep you abreast of this executive's availability. I was working with a major insurance company in Minnesota, and I had arranged to meet with the CEO to interview for this book. He had agreed, but in the meantime he accepted a new position with an even bigger company. Now I really wanted to talk with him. Unfortunately, he was extremely busy and I was getting nowhere. So I used my Golden Network and we strategized how I could get into his schedule.

You may also rationalize that the executive has delegated the responsibility to a lower level person you are working with. Executives delegate because they don't want to do the legwork. They do not delegate the responsibility because they can't. This is their job. They let someone else gather all the details and make a recommendation to them. Executives decide. Subordinates recommend. What would happen if the recommendation was in your favor, but the executive had a relationship with your competitor?

Another reason the executive may not want to see you is that he doesn't want to be sold. You wouldn't want to see someone that wants to sell you, either. Therefore your focus must be on sincerely understanding and helping this executive. If so, your approach will indicate this and your chances of success will be high. If this is about selling or convincing, you'll get nowhere.

Once again, use your Golden Network to get you an introduction to this executive. However, prepare. Determine what this executive wants from you – not vice versa. When he gets what he wants, you'll get what you want and not before.

CHAPTER 11

Obstacle 5
The Decision Has Been Delegated and It Is Unnecessary to See the Executive

This is a rationalization even if you have convinced yourself or some subordinate has convinced you that it is unnecessary to see the executive. Remember that executives make decisions. Subordinates do the legwork and influence the executive. Additionally, executives influence each other and their whispers at lunch or in the boardroom are very powerful. Again, what if your competitor was connected with some other executives in the executive suite? What would that mean to you? Would you be concerned?

Therefore it is always necessary to focus on getting to the executives and as many as you can. The more who know you the more you can turn to for information and introductions to help you with first and follow-on sales.

This is the obstacle that has cost me the most sales and has wasted most of my time. Somehow I don't want to put in the energy to network to the executives or a subordinate has made it clear that the decision rest with him or her. In my heart and brain I know better, but I get sucked in. The reason I have been made to feel it is unnecessary is that someone is hiding something. That something has killed me and it will kill you. Either another competitor is connected with the subordinate or executives, or maybe there is no desire by upper management to pursue this.

When executives are willing to talk to you, you will get the story – good or bad. You can then decide what to do. When you are not able to speak to these decision-makers and powerful influences, you are in trouble.

Even if you get the sale, without getting to and spending interview time with executives, you will not have a clear advantage for the next sale or a peripheral sale. Then, God forbid, if something happens during the implementation and you have no executive to talk with for advise or support, you're dead.

While writing this book all three of these incidents happened to me. I'm not proud of it, but it happens. I got complacent and I lost. How will you roll the dice?

Sleep on it.

CHAPTER 12

Obstacle 6
You're Not at the Executive's Level

L evel is all about credibility. It may be easier for a Sr. VP of your company to get to a VP of your customer's company because of the power and credibility of the office. However, just like anybody else, your executives have the capability to screw up deals and meetings. The title gives them the credibility and it is theirs to lose the second they open their mouth.

Executives will see people who have credibility with them. People they trust. If the subordinate has it, the executive will see the subordinate for the information. If you have it, you can deliver your message. It doesn't matter what your title. Executives want to see people they can trust to deliver and not waste their time. So long as he has credibility it could be the janitor.

Therefore you must gain credibility and here is where you can use your Golden Network big time. These people can get you an introduction to the executive because the executive trusts their judgment. You will then have the chance to develop your own credibility, or lose it, the second you open your mouth. Therefore, you must prepare before you meet the executive. What value will you bring? How will you show your professionalism? What will cause him to respect you so that he will listen to you? How can you earn credibility? What can you do so he will trust you to deliver and not waste his time? The people on your Golden Network can help you here, too.

Level is also about your confidence or lack of confidence. If you are confident, you exude confidence and you appear more credible initially. As noted, successful salespeople are confident and thus there is never a concern about being at the wrong level. Are they anxious or uncomfortable? Many times they are. However, their confidence carries them through. A little later, we'll discuss getting confidence.

CHAPTER **13**

Obstacle 7
The Embedded Competitor

One of the biggest deterrents to me is an account that is already using my competitor. However, this is my personal hang-up because it is actually the biggest opportunity for business. This account has already committed to using my types of services, so the need is established and this is a big plus. Additionally, competitors always have weaknesses that will cause dissatisfaction. Finally it is always easier, as the underdog, to work your way to the top than it is to stay at the top. Staying at the top requires constant attention, and most salespeople let the existing accounts cruise on autopilot while they pursue new opportunities. This becomes your opportunity because there are always chinks in the competitors' armor and those chinks are benefits that the customer isn't getting that they would like to have.

The strategy to deal with an embedded competitor is, again, develop a relationship with executives. They will want to see you because things are always changing and their needs are changing. There are always new projects. There are always likes and dislikes of the incumbent competitor. You need to know these because this tells you what they like that they are getting and what they want that they are not getting.

With embedded competitors it is extremely important to reach executives because only they can approve change. Subordinates don't want to go through the hassle of change. They would rather live with the devil they know. Executives usually cause and approve change, so this is where you have to be.

The strategy to deal with an embedded competitor is to position yourself as the number two supplier for this account. Set yourself up with these executives so that when these chinks, changes, or unmet needs start to create desire, you're considered first. Besides, the constant turnover of personnel in today's business world opens the door for the number two supplier continuously. Changes will be coming. If you're on top, you have to work hard to stay there. Most companies or salespeople don't implement strategies to maintain position. This creates the opportunity for number two.

Other reasons to be number two are that there may be room for more than one supplier. The company may not want all its eggs in one basket and/or one supplier may not have the breath of solutions to cover all of the needs. Most suppliers are strong in certain areas and not as strong in other areas; yet, the customer wants the best in all areas. So there usually is opportunity, and the best way to take advantage is to get to the executives.

Executive relationships will get you sales and more sales either directly or indirectly, either now or in the near future. With embedded competitors you may not have much of a Golden Network, so you will have to start a network first. Look back to the section where we discussed developing a network. Open your mind. How can you get involved? You know people who know people. Who will you ask for help? There is plenty of information available. How will you start digging?

A client of mine was sitting next to an executive on a plane not too long ago and they got into a conversation about a business book one of them was reading. One thing led to another and they started talking about consultants. Well, my name came up and they had a discussion about me. My client called me and gave me this other executive's name and the reason he would like to talk to me, so I called. After a discussion, it was clear that they were involved with a training group for salespeople, yet there were some changes under way and training was going to take a new direction. This new direction – 'executive relationships' – was not covered in the current curriculum or in their practical world. It took me a while, however. I used the first executive to get me to other executives so that I could establish relationships. The first executive was moved to another position even before I could sell anything, but I had already established a foothold to leverage. Finally I got some business. My initiative now is to continue networking, to establish a Golden Network so as to get more and more of their business.

The point that needs emphasis is that with embedded competitors you have to get to the executives because the lower levels will have no reason to see you. They follow orders and avoid any changes from the outside. Executives create change and are open to ideas that will help them get to where they need to be to stay ahead of their competition. However, to know what and why they want to see you, you need help – your network. Go in cold and you'll get nowhere but frustrated.

Workshop

Select an executive that you'd like to meet but cannot get to. Who is the executive? What's the reason? 1–Don't know who; 2–Blocked; 3– I'm uncomfortable; 4–No reason to see me; 5–Unnecessary; 6–Wrong level; 7–Competitor embedded. What will you do about it? Sleep on it.

Section III

Preparing for
the Meeting

CHAPTER 14

Credibility
The Magic of Any Relationship

Credibility is the force of attraction in a relationship. It is the reason an executive will meet you. It is why the executive believes s/he can win with you. It is the essential component behind the sale.

Do I respect you? Can I trust you? Can you deliver results? This is what the executive is saying to herself, consciously or unconsciously, whenever you try to interact with her. There are different levels of credibility, but these three criteria are always present and will determine whether you reach the next highest level. What holds you back from reaching a higher level on the pyramid is failure in either respect, trust, and/or results. *Figure X (page 80)* shows the different levels of credibility.

What can you do to get 'yes' answers to these questions? This is the start to developing credibility. Continuing to ask that question will enable you to develop ongoing strategies and tactics to establish and improve your credibility.

Figure X

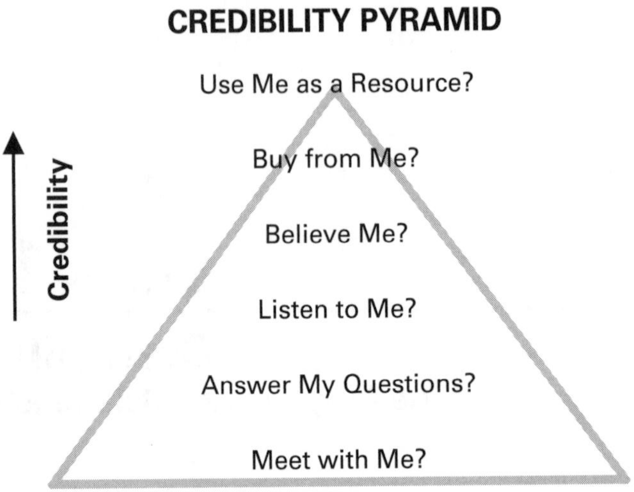

CREDIBILITY PYRAMID

Use Me as a Resource?

Buy from Me?

Believe Me?

Listen to Me?

Answer My Questions?

Meet with Me?

Credibility ↑

Credibility is between you and the person you are talking to. It is not about your company, although company credibility can help or hurt your credibility. Credibility has to be earned and this takes interaction and effort. Successfully delivering results is the best way of earning credibility. If you haven't had a chance to earn credibility, your fallback position is to use your Golden Network for a referral. This is called transferred credibility. Transferred credibility will probably get you a meeting, and this is your start to earn respect and trust and to move up the pyramid. Isn't this what we say to others, or ourselves: "If I only had a chance to meet her, then I could show her that I can be trusted to deliver results." Well now you know how to do it. Sleep on it and you'll figure out the details.

Without earned or transferred credibility you will have to figure out what you can do to get anyone to respect, trust, and believe you can deliver results in order to get a meeting. Sure I'd like to call and use a crisp message and get right through or get a call back. The chances of this are slim or not at all. It's because you don't have credibility. The executive doesn't know you, so why should she respect you? You've never met, so how can she trust you? You haven't done anything for her because of the two previous issues, so how does she know you can deliver results. Bottom line, why meet with you? There are many who want to see her.

Without earned or transferred credibility you have to use what you have – your professionalism, your associations, your knowledge, and your experience. Use yourself – your personality, your demeanor, your appearance, your sensitivity, your thoughtfulness. You have to use whatever will get you some respect and make an impression to get you started. This will take different levels of effort depending on who you start with. An admin might merely have to see you or feel comfortable with your tone or message. A subordinate may need a presentation, a demonstration, a plant tour, and a guarantee. Getting through the voice mail of an executive is going to require a message about what is important to this individual at this moment and linking this to someone she trusts and believes. Even if you get through and talk to a live exec, your chances of getting a commitment from this person to take any kind of action for you is remote. In my mind action is success – action to see you, action to refer you to another person, action to review your materials and give you feedback. The success rate is low because of no credibility.

The easiest way to establish credibility is to use your Golden Network. These people can introduce you to admins and execs and get you through some blocks. They will give you the opportunity to start working on establishing credibility. Then it is yours to lose as soon as you open your mouth. However, they can give you critical information to prepare you for the meeting. They can give you pertinent information to use on the voice mail. They can also call the exec to introduce you so that when your voice mail gets to the exec, she listens and gets back to you.

Developing credibility with subordinates requires much more work. But again, your Golden Network can help you strategize on what you have to do to move up the pyramid with a particular subordinate. Your Golden Network can help you learn what it takes to earn respect, trust, and results, as well as how to make this person comfortable with you.

Without a Golden Network your best alternative to start the credibility journey is to use your base-level network. Take the time to open your mind and do the digging of who you know who can help you. Otherwise you have to establish credibility on your own and this is the toughest. You will have to explain to the blockers what you have that would help them believe you and trust you so that you can get through to someone who counts. You might say something about your background, your experience in their industry, people you know who they know, things you've done that are important to them. The more personal you get, the better. Have you done something they asked you to do? – remind them. For example, did they ask you to send some literature? Remind them that you did what was asked – not for payback but because you are reliable. Mention areas of common interest: kids, hobbies, your education, successful projects you've done for others.

A subordinate blocker will start listening to you if she feels comfortable with you and believes you have the background, education, and experience for her to take the time to talk to you. In other words, "Do I respect, trust, and believe I can gain something and/or not lose anything from spending time with you?" It will also depend on the person's style. She may want you to be personable, or to the point. You'll need to be able to read what her style is. We'll cover this a little later.

Moving up the pyramid requires constantly providing respect, trust, and results. Will she meet with you? If yes, then she respects you, trusts you will be worth her time, and expects results. If she won't meet you, you have failed in one or more element: respect, trust or results. The same is true all the way up the pyramid. Will she decide to buy from you? If 'yes,' you've established credibility at this level. If not, you've failed in respect, trust, and/or results. Will she use you as a resource to protect or enhance her position? 'Yes' means you have established credibility and you now have the basis for a relationship. 'No' means you have to learn where and how you've failed, and then correct it.

CHAPTER 15

Confidence
A Salesperson's Biggest Asset

Talking to executives also requires confidence. As we mentioned before, if you're confident, you exude confidence and people, especially executives, pick up on it. If you are positive, feel secure about talking to this executive and feel comfortable about yourself in this situation, your chances of going further with this executive goes up exponentially. When you ask questions, your executive will respond in a meaningful way. When you speak, your executive will listen and take action. Confidence is a salesperson's biggest asset.

Confidence is not arrogance. There is a difference.

Confidence – You believe in yourself.

Arrogance – You are full of yourself.

Confidence – You believe in what you have to offer.

Arrogance – You believe you are the offer.

Confidence – You believe you can help this executive.

> Arrogance – You know you can sell this executive.
> Confidence – You realize this executive wants help.
> Arrogance – You know you can convince this executive.
> Confidence – It's OK to walk away.
> Arrogance – You will not give up.

Confidence doesn't mean being aggressive, either. The two are mutually exclusive. A confident person could be aggressive, or not. Just as an aggressive person may be confident, or not. Confidence means you're secure with who you are, what you've got, and where you are. Aggressive means you attack.

Getting Confident

There are three ways to become confident: (1) Learn what you have to do, (2) Prepare for the situation, and (3) Prepare yourself.

Tiger Woods is an extremely capable and confident golfer. His mission is to stay in range of the leaders and if possible get head to head with the leader on Sunday afternoon. He is confident he can win. When Tiger is close to the leaders, most competitors screw up the games that got them to the top of the leader-board. They lack the confidence to stay within themselves and play their game. They grow intimidated (which destroys confidence) because of the reputation and successes of Tiger Woods. This is a double plus for Tiger and a double minus for his competitors.

Now Tiger has learned and continues to learn his trade. He has been practicing and training with coaching since he was three. Bryon Nelson, one of the greatest golfers, says Tiger's work ethic is what sets him apart. Nobody practices as much as he does. Tiger continuously gets coaching from Butch Harmen so that he practices corrective and good habits. (Practicing bad habits reinforces the bad habits, which leads to worse conditions.)

Tiger also prepares for events. I remember hearing that in preparation for the 1997 Masters – his first major win – he practiced putting on a wooden gym floor because the greens at Augusta were so fast and hard. Before and in-between rounds he will spend more time chipping and putting than on the driving range in order to get a feel for the grass and conditions of this course. He walks the course with his caddie and practices shots he feels will come in play because of the conditions of this course. Then, when he is confronted with a tough situation, he's confident because he's well prepared for it.

Tiger also prepares himself mentally and physically. One attribute of his success is his ability to prepare mentally. He uses a good deal of eastern cultural mental preparation. His mother is from Thailand and has taught him to meditate and develop a calmness that leaves him comfortable with the situations at hand. He also does aerobic and weight training to physically condition himself for the endurance and strength required to stay sharp during a tough match.

Learning Your Job

Learning the correct behaviors and habits of selling is critical for your success and confidence as a salesperson. It's important to realize and acknowledge this. You never learned the correct behavior for selling. You certainly didn't study it in college. You probably picked it up yourself through the school of hard knocks. Think about the people who learned golf as kids compared to those who started as adults. Tiger started at two years old.

Learning about selling is poorly handled in most businesses. It is usually left to the individual to figure it out. Some companies train, but most don't offer on-going coaching or implementation follow-up. This is the reason only some seven and a half percent of the people trained actually use the training. Very few companies have coaching and implementation programs, and then they wonder why the three-day training event didn't produce for them. It is impossible to coach yourself effectively.

Most companies have product training, which is usually run by the Marketing Department. Again seven and a half percent of the people leave with a good knowledge of the products. The rest leave with the message that they need to *tell* about the products/services and that these are better than those of the competitors. Little is discussed about the process of selling. The salesperson goes out and tells the world and gets rejected, all because people don't want to be told, cajoled or convinced. This rejection feedback then goes toward building negative confidence and poor self worth. The salesperson blew it but doesn't know why and blames himself for not being capable. Then, this spirals down and down as a sense of low self worth sets in. They tend to rationalize about price and competition, but the loss hurts and leads to negative feelings that destroy confidence.

Learning requires studying, getting coached, trying, assessing, getting more coaching, correcting, and trying again. The process continues forever.

Preparing for the Situation

Just as Tiger walks the course or takes practice shots from various locations, you too must prepare for the situation. It is a simple yet highly effective way to build confidence in selling. Gather as much information as you can about the person or people you'll be with before the meeting. Review it with your team, associates, or your manager for more information, ideas, and actions. Think of times when you've had pre-call reviews with your team before important meetings. You probably felt pretty confident going into the sales calls. This is similar to preparing for an exam. When you prepared you felt a whole lot better than when you hadn't prepared. Without preparation you probably felt nervous and afraid of doing poorly. Fear destroys confidence.

Whenever I have a meeting, I call the people inside and outside the account who know the people who will be in the meeting. I try to gather as much information about the individuals and the problems, issues opportunities, etc., as I can. Then I call the people directly and ask them, one on one, their expectations of the meeting. I say, "I'm just calling to confirm our meeting and to learn your expectations of the meeting so that I can prepare and not bore you with grizzly details that you don't care about. So, what are your expectations for this meeting?" Then I listen and take notes.

I usually have the person who arranges the meeting warn everyone who I will call that I'm going to call. This gets me past voice mail and admins. If I set it up myself, I make sure I ask this expectation question before I end the set-up call. This pre-meeting call is extremely powerful. I learn a great deal about the person and his/her issues, situation, opportunities, wants, etc. It also establishes a rapport between us. The person knows me a little better and I've shown professionalism and respect for his/her time. I certainly know the person better, and when I meet him/her in person it is invariably more cordial and friendly. We've established mutual interest and the conversation is more advanced. Before we begin, I confirm the expectations and let the person or people clarify or elaborate further. I then present very targeted features and benefits that go to each person's issues and opportunities.

Another thing I do before the meeting is a sales call plan. I learned how to build a good one years ago through Miller Heiman, Inc., and it proved to be so successful that I will not go on a sales call without taking the 10 minutes to prepare it. Once I put it together, I am prepared and focused. I know what I have to learn. I'm prepared to present what's important to each person in a way that differentiates me from the competition. I'm also prepared to ask for commitment and to deal with objections or issues. This preparation is extremely effective for making me feel confident. The person or people feel this confidence and it's easy to move forward. With this kind of preparation you go in with the confidence of knowing what has to be done as opposed to the anxiety of seeing what you can find out.

Therefore, to build confidence, *prepare for the situation* before the meeting. Learn about the people from others and learn about the people from them directly. Finally, always prepare your sales call plan.

Prepare Yourself

Confidence is the feeling of being capable and worthy of the situation. We are confident in some situations and not confident in others. We are not born confident. We develop confidence by the way we are raised. However, we can build confidence by taking some conscious steps.

Preparing yourself may require more work – work you may not be willing to face. Confidence comes from within – getting over self-doubt. Self-doubt is believing you are not capable or not worthy of seeing an executive. Since you know it is not about capability – you have the capability – it must be about how you feel about yourself: *not worthy*. We tend to put influential decision-makers on power pedestals because they control the decision to buy. You have been conditioned that this person is important and this establishes fear. You've also been conditioned that this important person doesn't want to spend her valuable time with you. Thus as noted, you start believing that you are not worthy.

However, if she has expressed a need for help and if you have something that can help this person, she will want this information. She may have delegated this to a subordinate, but remember delegation just means do the legwork. She will make the final decision and has to get the information from someone. That someone should be you. You are capable and worthy of meeting with her. Keep in mind that she has a job just as you do. She has challenges as you do, and like you, she needs someone to help her with her issues. That someone should be you because you are capable of helping her.

Confidence also comes from *positive* projection. Make positive statements to yourself and others such as, "This interview will go great," and believe it. See yourself relaxed and having a calm positive conversation with this executive. You need to stay positive. Say to yourself and others, "Even if she doesn't want what I have, it's OK," and believe it. "She may not be ready for change. This is her state of mind. It has nothing to do with me," and believe it. "She has other priorities." "She's already developed a relationship with someone else. So what? People have multiple relationships," and believe it.

The key is to go in positive and this will keep you confident. If you go in with the thought that you have nothing to lose, you've already lost. You have no confidence, only failure, and you create your destiny – the eventual failure. In the future think about the best that can come out of this meeting and the minimum you're willing to accept from this person. If you don't get your minimum, you're going to spend your time elsewhere. You're not a failure if you don't get this person to meet with you or to change or to give you the order. This is only one of many people you do business with. You have other opportunities and options.

Babe Ruth struck out a lot. Joe Montana threw interceptions. The Williams sisters lose their serves in a tennis match. Tiger Woods hits shots into the water, ruff, and sand traps. Nowhere along the way did they, or do they, feel incapable or not worthy of the task at hand. They were secure or comfortable. They may have also been nervous, but that's healthy and normal. They just worked harder and got pumped up for the next situation.

Positive self worth, positive projection, and getting pumped up will have to come from you. So how do you get there? Well, the following is a method to get you confident.

CHAPTER 16

Your Trinity
Gain Confidence,
and Overcome Self Doubt

Lack of confidence, self-doubt, and low self-esteem come from negative talk within yourself. This negative talk was programmed into you as a child. See, it was your parents or friends or significant adult influences that programmed you. However, that was then. Now, it is you who chooses to hold on to these programs – even if they don't serve you. You can change this just as you have changed other beliefs in your life. For example, you probably don't believe that cleaning off your plate at meals will affect starving children in China or Africa. However, you may still believe that you never finish what you start; or that you are always causing problems; or that you will never amount to anything.

This childhood programming is your biggest asset and obstacle in life. It can help you succeed and hold you back from attaining all you are capable of being. Hold on to what serves you and notice what doesn't, because the negative programming that holds you back can be changed, and here is how it works.

There are three significant components within you that control your life, your thoughts, your attitude, etc. They are your child, your parent, and your spirit.

Your Child

The child in you is responsible for your feelings. Those feelings are mad, sad, glad, afraid, ashamed and hurt. When something happens to you, good or bad, it is your child that reacts. The child is in charge of your feelings. For example, someone says a negative thing to you and you react. The child is feeling mad, sad, glad, afraid, ashamed, and/or hurt – any combination, any number. In this instant let's say you feel mad, hurt, and afraid. Mad because it's not true. Sad because it was mean. Hurt because you trusted this person. The child in you feels this and reacts. It will *act-in* – pout, cry, become depressed or *act-out* – say something in retort, yell, take a punch, or storm out.

Now most people are not even aware of their feelings. Let's take a test. How do you feel right now – mad, sad, glad, afraid, ashamed, hurt? Those are the only choices. Please don't argue with me that there are more feelings. This is from the psychologists. Argue with them.

So what are you feelings? Mad, Glad, Sad, Afraid, Ashamed, Hurt. Ask yourself, "Am I feeling mad?" If no, continue with "Am I glad?" and so on. If yes, ask yourself what's causing this. Take a second to ask yourself, and then wait and listen to yourself. Go ahead and try.

As I'm writing, I'm feeling glad (happy) that I'm working on my book and that I have a life that lets me do it. I'm sad because it is taking so long, and I'm afraid that I won't meet my deadlines. My reactions are to keep working and take a break in a few hours. If I get a phone interruption, I'll probably be terse and abrupt – my child will be acting out. The call will slow me down – remember I'm afraid.

TRINITY
Confidence, Self Esteem, Getting What you Want

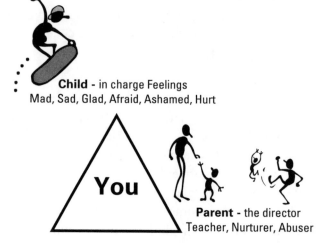

Child - in charge Feelings
Mad, Sad, Glad, Afraid, Ashamed, Hurt

You

Parent - the director
Teacher, Nurturer, Abuser

This is the world of my child. It's talking to me and unless I make a conscious effort to listen to it, I will not know what it is saying. I will only be reacting.

Your child has not been programmed. This is the real you. So if you want to know who you are and what you really want from and for yourself, start talking and listening to your child. Ask what you're feeling and listen. This will take a little work, but it's worth it.

Your Parent

The parent in you is the director. It is your guide, your coach, your teacher, your protector, and more. It nourishes you and can abuse you. For example, I would really like to play golf right now – child in me wants to play. However, I have to work on this book – parent guiding me. This is good up to a point. If I start spending 15 hours a day for many days writing in order to get the book finished on time, this is abusive. My parent after a point has to say, "Let's take a break. Let's play." This is nourishing. Now how does your parent learn how to parent, guide, protect, and direct you? It learned or was programmed by your real parents or significant influences in your youth. That little voice in your head telling you what to do is your parent that is mimicking your real parents.

Remember I said that self doubt or lack of confidence is negative talk within you. It is coming from the parent within you that was programmed by your life parents and other influences. Now did they mean to warp you? – I'll say 'no.' However, perhaps they didn't know what they were doing. They didn't know any better. Their parents, who probably messed them up worse, programmed them. Then they passed their programming down to you. They didn't mean to negatively affect you, and in many ways, they positively programmed you. However, that's what you got and that's history. Unfortunately, it left some scars and for sure some negative programming within you.

So how do you get rid of the negative voice or any other baggage you're carrying? You first take note of what you're feeling. Believe me, this will take some concentration. Try it again. What are you feeling as you read this – Mad, Sad, …? Maybe annoyed (mad) and anxious (afraid)? Why? Does it serve you? If not, do you want to change? If yes, you must turn to your coach, protector, guide (your parent) and say, "Let's change the program. It's not serving me." "Parent, make it happen."

Now your parent will probably say, "Well how am I going to do that?" This is where you turn to your spirit. Ask yourself, "What can I do?" You will get an answer. Try it. Ask yourself what you can do about a problem you are facing. Stop and listen to yourself. You will get an answer or an idea. This comes from your spirit. This is where the "Sleep on it" principle comes from. Ask yourself what you can do. Give it some time. Then listen. Answers will come, and they come from your spirit through to your parent.

Your Spirit

The spirit is your enabler. It is responsible for your motivation, your creativity, your problem-solving capabilities, your clairvoyance, your inspiration, and more. The spirit kicks in

TRINITY
Confidence, Self Esteem, Getting What you Want

Child - in charge Feelings
Mad, Sad, Glad, Afraid, Ashamed, Hurt

You

Spirit - the enabler
Motivation, Inspiration,
Clairvoyance

Parent - the director
Teacher, Nurturer, Abuser

when activated by you. It is like a spell check on your computer. It will auto correct some words, and when asked, will check the whole document. However, first you have to ask it.

The same applies to you. If you ask yourself to change, your spirit will kick in and give you alternatives, options, and suggestions. It can enable your parent to start leading you in a new direction. It will give you the insights to write a plan that directs you. It's all there for the asking.

Now if your child is afraid (feeling) to take the chance, then ask your parent what you are afraid of. What program (voice) is cautioning you? What negative outcome are you projecting? Then, ask yourself (spirit) what you can do? Sleep on it and the answers will come.

So get rid of the negative talk. Tell your parent you want positive talk. Then ask your spirit, "How can I make this happen?" Sit back, listen, and start writing. Your child will feel fear from the answer, but your parent must rally to protect and nurture your child. So you ask yourself, "How will I overcome my fear?" Sit back, listen, and start writing. Sometimes it takes the spirit awhile to respond or to show you the way. But the answer is within you and the time required to get it out will depend on all the layers of defense that have to be penetrated. The answer may be as simple as go talk to someone for advice. That advice may stimulate your spirit to create other ideas and suggestions.

Think of those awesome statements about how important people are or how powerful they are. These statements and hundreds of others like them built your program. Then when your boss, or as I'm saying now, says, "Get to the senior executive," your child reacts from fear (discomfort). The parent has instructed: "Proceed with caution or stay away." Your spirit gives you the rationalizations, creative excuses to procrastinate, stay away, and survive. I have worked with so many people who truly believe that getting to an executive is unnecessary. They can explain in such detail and use lots of energy to try and convince me. As I work with them, they finally admit it is possible and difficult; but getting them to admit is a struggle. The child is afraid. The parent is advising the child. The spirit is enabling.

Try this exercise. If your son or daughter or a close friend came to you explaining his or her reluctance to see a boss or corporate executive, what advice would you give? Can you give yourself the same advice?

If you can't give yourself the same advice or if you rationalize why it is different for you – you have self-worth issues. Go through the exercises previously described.

Self-worth and self-doubt are the negatives of confidence. Someone along the line gave you negative programming about your abilities. Your child was hurt because it knew that the negatives are wrong – "I am capable." However, your child is also afraid to refute this, "These are the people that love me and they would never do anything to hold me down." Your parents were instilling fear because they were probably afraid. The parent has to protect, train, advise, and do all the things that parents do. This is how they handled it. Parents can be supportive or abusive. It really depends on their issues. Holding you down by stating negatives may have helped them handle their fear. Unfortunately, you picked up a different message.

In like manner, the reverse happens. Think of your life. You have done plenty of good things – you graduated, you got a job and held it, you have friends, you make sales, you do acts of charity at home and/or in the community. You've done plenty to be proud of yourself. You know you're good and worthy of anyone. That's your child speaking and s/he is happy. Now your parent has to support this. Your self-esteem is high and your child is happy. Have you ever noticed some people always seem to stay positive and make things happen?

Now your parent can be abusive and put you down by saying, "You're not that good. Look at all the mistakes you've made. You'd better not make any waves." Unfortunately, your parent kicks in automatically and self-doubt is perpetuated. Your child feels hurt. If it continues, the hurt turns to anger because your child knows it has worth and starts to act-in or act-out. This is why you see people blow up when you say something. You've hit a nerve. You've repeated the negative their parent has said to them. Now you've said it and the child has someone to act-out on. The child can also handle it by numbing the feeling – drinking, gambling, eating, and/or other addictions.

So self-doubt is something that's been programmed from your external parents and supported by your internal parent. Your external parents were cautious. Your external parents may have put you down. Your external parents may have done any number of negative things to you. This feedback and treatment formed your opinion about yourself. There's no sense lamenting. That was then and that's what happened. However, there is much you can do to improve your attitude about yourself now.

Since your external parents who were full of caution and put-downs programmed your internal parent, you have to reprogram your internal parent into a supportive element of your being. You do this by rallying your spirit. Talking to your spirit. You've done it all your life. Some call it self-talk – positive or negative. Some pray. Others meditate.

Prayer is the method I use. Meditation and self-talk are the same. Let me explain how it works. When I pray, I talk to myself. I may also be talking to the Transcendental God, but that is another topic which is about faith. This is not about faith. What I know for sure is that when I pray, meditate, or positive self talk, I am talking to myself. My spirit absorbs these requests and starts generating ideas, energy, and drive (while I'm sleeping on it). My spirit calls-out a path to get me what I am praying for. It is a plan. The parent starts directing me into areas and situations that helps me get what I want. Unfortunately it is not an abrupt, magical event with ghosts and visions. It is a series of actions that I take in a direction to make something happen. For example you want to become confident. So you start talking to yourself about the desire to be confident. Eventually, you plead internally, "Oh let me be confident and self-assured. I really want to be confident." If you really mean it, you will start noticing that the actions you take and situations you get involved with are leading you in the direction you believe will make you confident. Maybe you'll prepare more. Maybe you'll start networking to learn more and gain introductions. You have the answers. You just have to give them a path to come out.

If prayer is not your thing, there are many ways to talk to yourself to rally your inner strength or spirit.

W. Timothy Gallwey wrote a series of books about the inner game of tennis, golf, etc. It was all about one element of yourself (Self I) talking to the other part of yourself (Self II). Many have written about this concept. *Think and Grow Rich* and *The Power of Positive Thinking* are books that get you to talk to yourself and to notice the negative talk that you use in your life and change it to positive. Most eastern religions and philosophies talk about getting in touch with your spirit. These concepts are about getting you on a path to accomplish what you want. Your child is the one driving the desire. Your parent is the one sending out the instructions – hold back or full speed ahead. Your spirit is the engine that can make you go or hold you back. Remember the spirit enables what the parent asks it to do. If the parent give the instructions to step on the accelerator, you will speed ahead. If it says step on the break, you will slow down or stop. The parent gives instructions based on the program instilled from your upbringing. Now only you can change the program (redirect the parent) and care for your child by asking your spirit to make it happen.

Believe it or not you've been doing this subconsciously or unconsciously all your life. You wanted a job. Child wanted the benefits of money. Parent said, "You need employment." So you talked to yourself (spirit) and you asked, "What will I do?" or "Where will I work?" Somewhere along the line inspiration came (spirit) to your parent who directed you where to look, what to do, and who to call.

While writing this book, there were many moments (daily) when my child said, "I don't want to write today." My parent was saying, "You've got to do it." So my child cries out to the spirit, "How am I going to do this?" Parent says, "Sit down and start writing." Next thing I know I'm at the computer writing and thoughts are flowing.

Becoming Confident

As mentioned earlier, preparation is the key to building confidence. Prepare yourself and prepare your knowledge of the situation and the executive you will meet.

Preparing Yourself

Let's use the Trinity to prepare ourselves to be confident. Your child has to say, "I'm good." Your parent must support this feeling. "You are good, but you must prepare. Let's learn and prepare." Yet, you feel nervous and uncomfortable? Ask your spirit for help. Some say to themselves, "Oh Lord, help me." Others say, "What can I do?" Others stop and meditate and wait for inspiration. Whatever your style, become conscious of it. Use it in a positive way and it will happen. You have the responsibility to make yourself confident. You can rally your spirit and get your parent to work for and support you. However, you have to tell yourself that you want it and believe it.

I have a friend that is a mediocre golfer – 20 handicap, overweight, and not physically special. Occasionally during a match, he will stand on the tee and announce what a great athlete he is. Sure enough, he nails a drive long and straight into the middle of the fairway. What he's doing is talking to himself and rallying his spirit. While he is going through this drill, the rest of us are listening and shaking our heads in disbelief, but it doesn't matter. What does matter is that he is listening to himself. He is saying, "Spirit make this happen. Parent, visualize where it should go and the path to get it there." He then puts it into his spirit's world and lets it happen. When complete, his child is jumping for joy and razing us about his extraordinary capabilities. We just walk away with wonder and annoyance.

If you don't want to be confident, that's OK. You have made a conscious decision that it may take more energy, time and effort than you're willing to spend. Be sure this is conscious thinking and not rationalization, i.e., "I could never be confident about this. Therefore I don't want to be confident."

If you don't believe you can become confident, ask yourself, "Why? What was programmed in me that makes me believe I can't be confident about this situation? How come I can be confident in other situations?"

If you ask for confidence, you'll get it. However you have to listen for responses from yourself. If you ask, "What can I do?" – listen. You will get feedback. Keep calling on your spirit. Inspiration, motivation, directions, and luck will come. It may take some time and not flow as expeditiously as you'd like, but it will come. Have you ever heard the expression, "Things happen for the best?" They do, but they don't happen by themselves. You make those things happen. Your spirit inspires you. Your parent directs you. You pursue a new course that makes your child happy. Life is then good. If it's not, your child becomes unhappy and acts-in or acts-out.

Thus, before you approach a key executive or his blockers, you must prepare yourself. Get yourself in a state that says you are just as good a person as this executive. Studies have shown that DNA differences among individuals come to something like one hundredth of one percent. Thus we are 99.99% alike.

Invariably we get dressed the same way. The cloths may be different but the person is very similar. We all have a job to do. We all have priorities. We all have people to answer to. We all have goals, problems, and responsibilities. So, in lots of ways, you are like this executive.

Positively project that this regular person, this executive, will really appreciate what you have to offer. His staff of regular people will even help you get to this executive. Take everybody off the pedestals. Remove the weapon from their hands. Then, check your demeanor. Are you talking as a competent professional or as a timid beggar? Keep a mirror in front of you whenever making a phone call and check your expression. Do you look poised and confident or slumped and scared? Carry that thought with you when you are face to face.

How do you look when you order a pizza? What do you say? "Hi, I'd like to order a large, cheese and pepperoni pizza." How do you look when you talk to a key executive. What do you say when you call. "Hi, my name is Sam Manfer from Sam Manfer Sales Consultants and your interest in improving your salespeople's productivity has been brought to my attention.

Do you look the same? – Pizza person? Executive? You should. Prepare yourself mentally.

Preparing Your Knowledge of the Situation and Executive

Knowing about this executive and how your products/services affect this executive will help you be confident. Knowing the business issues that face this executive will also help you be confident. This preparation will get you familiar with the territory. It clears up the mystery and minimizes your negative projections. Think about an important sales call you and some of your company people went on. You and your people did some checking and information gathering with the account's people, and with your own organization. The team probably got together the night before the call and discussed who was going to say what. Who was going to ask specific questions?

What should we be looking for or listening for? How should questions be addressed? What are some of the known concerns? Where and what should be done to handle them? Much preparation went into this, but think how you felt the next day going into that room. I'll bet you felt solid and confident. Even if you were concerned about certain issues, you felt you could handle them. You were confident because you took the time and made the effort to learn about the person and the situation. You prepared.

Confidence will help you get and keep an executive's attention. It makes you believable and credible. However, it doesn't always mean you get through and captivate the executive or get the order. However your chances for success are greatly improved. More importantly, if it doesn't go well, you will be able to analyze it objectively and move on without blaming yourself. Without confidence you tend to take it personally and seek safety. Your child is hurt and afraid. The next endeavor will be in jeopardy.

So to get yourself confident, sense your feelings. If you're not happy, and feeling afraid, ask yourself, "Why?" Then tell your parent to change this. If your parent doesn't know how to do it or reprogram, then rally your spirit by asking for help. Then sleep on it. It will come in one form or another.

Section IV

Talking to an Executive

CHAPTER **17**

Productive Executive Discussions

PRODUCTIVE EXECUTIVE DISCUSSIONS

So now we have overcome any obstacle to get to the executive and we are confident and prepared to talk with the executive, what will we say and talk about to make this all worthwhile.

It's All About the Executive

Always remember that the issues are all about the executive. If you forget this point you will blow yourself apart. So let's focus on the executive.

Party Line Issues

Party line issues are topics, issues, results, solutions, etc., that people and their associates talk about in public. These center on the corporate mission, corporate initiatives and issues senior management has declared important. These are safe topics to discuss in public because everybody is on the same party line. For example, "We are making an all out effort to reduce costs and be the leaders in the market place." This is a corporate mission. Although interested in these topics, the

EXECUTIVE FOCUS

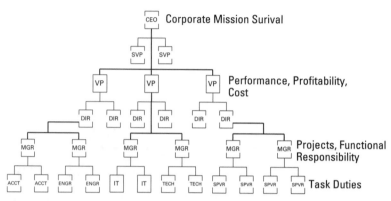

Figure Y

individual executive is very focused on the particular issues that relate to him, to his department, and/or his agenda. If you start telling this individual how you can help with lower cost and market leadership, and it's not his hot button, you will hear – "But, but, but..." or passive resistance, "Sure, isn't that great! What else?" You will lose this executive because you're not coming close to what is important to him. Have you ever noticed when you call someone after reviewing the annual report and recite back much of that information, you get a lukewarm or cold reception? It's because you've missed the target for this person and/or every other vendor has already used that line.

Levels and Interest

Let's look at the Organization chart – *Figure* Y and the Product Impact vs. Company Size – *Matrix 1, pg. 43.* Ask yourself what impact does my product have on this company? Who will I be talking with? What's his level? What's his focus? You may be meeting Engineers, System Analysis, Accountants, Supervisors, Manager, VP's, Senior VP's, C's and Presidents, Owners, and/or Board Members. All have focus, responsibilities, and hot buttons that could be very different from each other's.

Lower Levels

Lower level people don't make the decision, however, they may be important to the decision making process. They influence the executive decision-maker and they may have significant impact on the decision. So they could be important. These people are responsible for tasks and duties – that is, get the job done, on time, at the right rate, within the budget, etc.

Mid Levels

Managers are mid level and this is where executives start to reside. A manager's focus is projects or functional responsibility. That is, the new software system implementation, the new office building, the accounting department, the engineering department, customer service, Northeast sales, the HL 2004 product introduction are all examples of managers' responsibility. They want to know how you can help them do the project or how you can help make their department function better. Yes, they are concerned about the company mission. However, their hot button is their immediate domain, and personal information is not published anywhere.

The authority of mid-level managers is limited to smaller dollars or lower impact decisions. The size of the company will also determine the power. Now you may already be selling big dollars to this manager's department and this executive will affect your continued stream of income. He has power. However, he probably will not have the power alone to make a big dollar increase or a new, major impact decision. He does have the power to influence the decision, so his needs and wants will have to be addressed. He is important.

Mid-level managers will meet with each other but will not influence each other too much. There domain is theirs and unless what they are doing affects another manager's department, they act somewhat independent. For example, the accounting manager will not be listening to the engineering manager on accounting matters unless it is affecting the engineers' reporting and accountability. Even then the accounting manager will probably decide and the engineering manager will have to abide. This means that in their domain, managers are very powerful. But they don't have much power to make commitments for the company. So if you can help an engineering manager or operations manager do something better without additional money or resources, this manager will be the Power. If you can help but it requires an investment, the Power will be at a higher level.

This difference is important because salespeople think that because someone has the power to replace, with an "or equal," he also has the power to make an investment decision for change. He probably doesn't.

Upper Levels

CIOs, COOs, and VPs are upper level managers. This is where you should start to establish relationships. These people can make minor investment decisions, but their real importance to you is their proximity to the people who can make major investment decisions. VPs talk to each other before they make decisions. They eat lunch together. They check with each other before they commit to change. They are encouraged to team together. Even if there is infighting, these people know how to be politically correct and to be team players. They want top management to believe they can get along with each other. They meet regularly with the top managers and investment decisions are discussed as a team.

CIO's, COOs, and VPs are responsible for performance, profitability, costs, and business issues. For example, "Does the software and IT systems work effectively for information flow to the company and the customers? Are sales in the various regions at quota? Is the productivity high enough, the unit costs low enough, the product delivered on time? Are we keeping turnover low, hiring the right people and training properly?" These are examples of performance, profitability, and cost issues. These people want to know how you can help them with their area of responsibility. Their department is most important to them. They will ask, "How will your product/service directly impact me or the people who report to me?" If you explain to the CIO that his people will be less stressed and have an easier time with the implementation of the new software, he will not be as excited as he will be if you explain how start-up will be faster and inter-department confusion will be eliminated. See, stress and tough work is what his people are paid for. Fast start-up (performance) and no inter-department confusion (performance) are what *he's* paid for.

Top Levels

CEOs, CFOs, Sr. VPs are top level managers. Their focus is implementation of the corporate mission and corporate survival, once again as it relates to him/her. The Sr. VP Sales has to keep sales high to support levels of overhead, maintain market share and preempt competition. CFOs manage the acquisition process, the finances of the company and relations with the investment community. CEOs manage the survival or success of the company. "Do the existing systems support the investments for the future? In which direction should I be budging this company? How do I implement feedback from the Board of Directors and the investment community?"

Know these people – it's important. More importantly, they should know who you are and what your company does for them. It would be great if you had a professional relationship with these people, but be careful. These people may be too far removed from your services. This is especially true when you are dealing with a very large company. Check the Impact vs. Size *Matrix 1, pg. 43*. Does your product/service impact these people? Will subordinates discuss the decision to buy you or your competitor with one of these people? Will any of these people initiate the change that will utilize your products/services. If the answer is 'yes' to any, then you need to get connected and form relationships here.

I was working with a company that sold office supplies – pencils, paper, etc. Their people were challenged to go high in the organization. Their focus was the CFO. Tell me how many CFOs get involved in pencils and paper decisions? Not many and if they do they should be fired. Now if you were selling consulting services on how to improve relationships in the investment community, then the CFO would be a key player to have a professional relationship with. If your product/service requires big capital dollars or structural changes to existing processes, you'd be wise to have a relationship with the CEO and the CFO.

The Individual Executive

Executives are individuals and because of their rank and influence, they demand individualization more than others. So in order to talk with the executive you must talk about something that is important and interesting to this individual. You can obtain such information from people on your Golden Network, but some of that information may be a little off. You can get an executive upset with 'off' information. You'll lose your credibility in a heartbeat. So always be careful of the information you get from others. Use your Golden Network for an introduction and then become an investigative reporter to find out first hand what's important to this executive.

CHAPTER **18**

Asking the Questions
That Will Provide an Arsena
of Powerful Information

Executives love to talk about themselves, especially their professional world. This may be tough for you because you are not comfortable asking questions and letting people talk. You are probably more comfortable presenting. However, this will not get you pertinent information about this executive.

So to gather the most high quality information, you must start thinking of yourself as an *investigative reporter.* Investigative reporters interview people to get information. They ask questions and let the person talk. Investigative reporters also check and confirm that the information is correct. Once satisfied, they write their presentation – the story. However, before they interview they prepare. Think of some of the best reporters. My favorites are Ted Koppel, Diane Sawyer, Barbara Walters, Charlie Rose. They prepare before an interview. Yes they have a staff to gather public information and prepare a briefing. The staff also prepares a list of questions. But the star takes the time for the briefing and to edit the questions she will ask. In this way she will be able to ask set-up questions to get the person comfortable and establish rapport (credibility). As the interview progresses, they ask more pointed questions. Then, depending on the answers, they can go in many directions with follow-on questions. Bottom line, the interviewer is in control. The person being interviewed is revealing her inner most secrets in front of millions of people and feeling good about it. Notice, however, who is doing the talking.

In like manner you can be in control and get this key executive to tell you his innermost professional desires and what is important to him. He will love talking to you. He will tell you exactly what it will take to have a professional relationship with him. You will have an arsenal of ammunition to work with and he will show you exactly how to talk to him. The key is getting ready, asking and listening – not presenting.

Preparing for Your Interview

Get public information from all your sources and prepare questions to get the private information from your executive. Your sources for the public information are your Golden Network and the Internet. Your Golden Network can give you information about this executive – likes, dislikes interests, responsibilities, etc. The Internet has a wealth of information about the company from the company's perspective. Your interview – the questions you ask – will get you the private information.

Asking Questions

Asking questions can be a great technique or it can kill you. Your questions must be set up in a way that makes your executive feel comfortable and gives you the information you need. I'm sure you've been exposed to a salesperson – possibly real estate or a car dealer – where you went through "20-questions." That is, questions that were self-serving for the salesperson. S/he wanted to qualify you and you went along. You knew s/he needed to know something about you, but how did you feel? – probably aggravated. This person showed no concern about you and you probably blew her/him off – politely or whatever.

You don't want to aggravate or get blown-off, so structure your questions in a way that reflect your interest in learning about this executive for *his* reasons. That is, "Tell me about your situation so that I can understand the issues you're facing." The focus is on him and he will feel it. Feeling that you are sincere, he will start to open up a little to see how you handled what he's giving you. As long as he feels this is for him, he will help you with information. He'll keep telling you more and more because he's also figuring it out himself and he wants to give you everything so you can help him completely.

The executive will give you information because she knows you need it and that is why you are there. However, this concept may be revolutionary for a lot of salespeople. Executives know they have to give you information if they want help. They are willing to give it to you if you let them. Yet most salespeople feel they have to go in and give information. The irony is that unless an executive feels you understand her situation, she won't believe you know about her business or her. There is no way she is forming a relationship with someone who doesn't understand her situation and her. An example I like to use is a patient going to a new doctor. If you were prescribed a medication without the doctor asking any questions – or – if he asked only a few short, pointed questions and then prescribed, would you feel confident that he understood your condition? Would you feel he was prescribing correctly or would you feel he was pushing you through in order to get to the next victim? So even if you know all there is to know going in (which I guarantee you don't), your executive will not feel you understand her. Unless she has the opportunity to tell you about her situation and herself, she will figure it is all about you. Guess what? She doesn't care about you.

Frame Your Questions

Framing means asking in a manner that directs your executive to give you information important to you. The important criterion is to make him feel it is about him. Many times you'll ask a question about a personal occurrence such as a vacation or trip – just to be social. The executive goes off into detail after detail, which may or may not be interesting, but he is not giving you any usable information. You may have gotten into this situation by saying, "Tell me about your vacation." This leaves the option to the executive to go wherever he wants. If you just want to make him feel at ease with a pleasant opening about him, you might have asked, "Did you have a good vacation? Did it give you enough time away to relax?" Try short answer questions that break the ice.

When you get to more business oriented issues your questions have to be open ended and yet focused. You don't want short answers. You do want answers about his professional issues. Since I'm selling consulting services relevant to salespeople and sales managers, I might say "Tell me about your challenges getting forecast information from your sales team." I've now directed this executive to visualize his sales team and his forecast issues with them. If I said, "Tell me about your challenges making sales forecast." He could have focused on the unfairness of the forecast, the economy, the shortfalls of operations, lack of new products development, etc. This information might be interesting, but there is not much I can do about solving these issues. The part "from your sales team" focuses the attention there. Another way I might phrase a question to get what I want and make him feel it is about him would be, "Tell me what's working really well with your sales team." Let him answer. "What's not?" Let him answer. If you said, "Tell me about your sales team," who knows what you'd get? He may be very proud or busy and you'd get nothing of importance.

Know What You Want to Know

"Chance Favors the Prepared Mind,"
(*Under Siege II*, Steven Segal)

We've talked about asking questions and framing, but in order to do this and look professional you must know in advance what you want to learn from this executive. Now remember we are trying to develop a relationship with this executive – not sell him. Therefore our questions have to focus on learning about this individual and his or her world. The following are topics for discussion and an explanation of why you should explore them. This is not to say you'll be asking all of these. You are looking for information. As your executive answers an open-ended question, she will give you plenty of information. If your mind is attuned to what you want to know, you will pick it up and not need to ask all of these questions. If some specifics are missing, you can then ask a focused question. If you're not prepared, pertinent information will pass right over you.

Questions to Ask Regarding the Executive's World

Present Issues and Opportunities?

"Tell me about present issues and opportunities you are facing." These are current priorities and probably where her mind is focused.

The Future?

"What concerns do you have about the future of your company, your department, your position?" This is the vision or concerns of the CEO, the Board and her superiors. Fulfilling this vision, creating solutions to threats, and taking advantage of opportunities is her job with this company. She has worries, concerns, and anxieties dealing with these visions or issues. There may be something here that you can help with.

Attitude about Present and Future?

"How do you feel about the current situation?" – or about "The future vision of the company?" What are her likes/dislikes, worries, excitements, challenges? This will give you an understanding of what you have to work with. People act based on their feelings. If there is fear or disdain, there will be resistance to the whole initiative. Your actions will have to help her with her feelings – either commiserate or consult with her. If she is excited and happy, she will want to charge ahead.

Questions to Ask about the Executive Herself
Her Job?

How did she get into it? What were her expectations?
What are they now? Where does she want to go with
it? What is expected of her? If she accomplishes all that
is expected of her what will that do for her personally?
This will give you insights to what is driving her.
Helping her here will be where credibility is achieved
and where the relationship will start to bud.

How is she measured?

How will she know if she is doing a good job? What
measurable, tangible, quantifiable results will her boss
and her superiors use for evaluation? How will you
help her deliver these so that they are recognized? This
is how she will evaluate your relationship with her.

Her Risk Orientation?

Is she a risk taker or does she avoid risk? Ask about situations in the past to get an idea how she handled
them and what were the outcomes. What was she feeling when she was going through these situations?
What happened to her as a result? This will give you a
good idea of what she's feeling now. People can't feel
in the past. What she says will reflect her feelings now
– fear, happiness, anger, hurt, etc. This will be where
you will have to work to make her feel comfortable.
Otherwise, she will not move forward.

Alliances?

What does she think of her boss and other superiors?
Who are her supporters? Who does she have trouble
with – personally or with the vision? What about her
associates – supporters and detractors? What about
her subordinates? Who does she like to work with and
not work with? Why? This will give you insights to
how you will have to work with her. It will also let you
know what information or scuttlebutt from others to
repeat and what not to repeat.

Questions to Ask the Executives about Your Products/Services

What are her likes about your company, products, services?

What are her dislikes about your company, products, services?

What else does she want you to be doing?

What do you have to correct?

What additional features/services would she be willing to pay for – if available?

What can you and your company do to make her boss look good?

What can you and your company do to make her look better to her boss?

What can you do to make her subordinates look better to her?

How will she measure you and your company – measurable, quantifiable as well as subjective results?

What will make you succeed in her eyes?

What does she see or think of when your name is mentioned?

What does she see or think of when your company's name is mentioned?

Answers to the above questions will give you a good appreciation of where you stand with her. (Note: It's not the questions but the kind of information that these questions elicit that's critical.) Your assumption based on her actions will be misleading. The feedback from others will be inaccurate. Only her feedback will be a solid foundation to work from.

Questions to Ask the Executives About Your Competitors

What are her likes?

What are her dislikes?

How are others influencing her about your competition?

What political alliances and/or issues will be compromised working with or supporting you?

Now I don't expect you to go in and rattle off these questions. You'll be thrown out faster than the speed of light. However, I do expect you to be attuned to learning this information. Have a few open ended questions prepared. Focus them on the most important concerns for this conversation. Frame them to get her directed to where you want her to go and then listen to what she says. As you'll see in the next section, if you give them the opportunity then people will tell you a great deal from a well phrased question. As they click off information about the above topics, you can jot down the relevant points. If you haven't prepared to listen for this information, it will go right over your head. Worse yet, you'll hear something that is you-focused, blurt out and take over the talking. With this show of insensitivity, rudeness or stupidity, your executive will stop talking and figure out how to get away from you.

I was making a sales call with a very experienced medical salesperson at Scripps Hospital in the San Diego area. The salesperson started a conversation with a cardiologist, who happened to be in an administrative office. The cardiologist started to discuss the competition. He talked about something he liked. So this sales rep immediately started to tell him how her product had a feature that was better or whatever. Well, that cardiologist immediately said some pleasantry and was history. Had the rep let him talk, she would have learned so much. He probably would have stayed for a while and who knows what else could have happened. We'll discuss this behavior more in the next section.

CHAPTER 19

Getting the
Critical Information

In order to build your arsenal of ammunition, you will have to know with certainty what is important to this executive. In this section we will present the concept of listening, taking notes, understanding what is said, and confirming the meaning of the information.

Listening

After confidence, listening is the most valuable quality of a salesperson or anyone trying to form a relationship. A participant in one of my sessions recently made the comment, "The person doing the talking is having all the fun." This is so true. When I run sales workshops, I usually ask people why they talk so much and listen so little. The answers are usually:

I'm afraid of what the person might say. I won't be able to handle it.

I need to get my message out. The executive doesn't know all I can do.

I'm in control.

It takes too much time to let them do the talking.

In addition to the above, my spin on why people don't listen is: People don't care. More or less it is all about me.

Marketing has been the model for most salespeople and marketing is all about telling.

There are some misconceptions that need addressing. Being afraid of what someone might say is very real. However, you need to know about it. If it's positive, you'll want to use it. If it is negative, you won't get anywhere until it is dealt with. So you might as well get it out and deal with it. Fear of what they will say is based on negative projection. You don't know what this person will say, so what are you afraid of? Once he says it, you'll know the problem and you can deal with it.

Control is the worse misconception. When you are speaking/presenting, you have no control. The executive could be day dreaming or blowing you off in her mind. People can be very good at hiding what they're thinking. Recall my analogy of good investigative reporter getting people to reveal all on TV. Who's in control? – the person asking the questions or the person revealing?

"It takes too much time" is all about you. The same is true with the marketing approach. You want to tell what you've got or why you should have a relationship with the executive and expect that person to embrace you. As you've probably seen, it doesn't work that way. It's all about what's in it for the executive. You can present and hope he connects or you can ask him what's important and then connect what you have to his vision. The latter takes far less time, is more accurate, and lets you know quickly what you're in for. It also goes a long way to showing professionalism and sincerity, which is necessary to establish respect and trust – elements of credibility.

Golden Silence

This is a concept I learned while working with Miller Heiman, the sales training company, but the concept has been around since the beginning of communications. This will be the most powerful and useful concept you will ever deploy. It works in business as well as in your personal life. It is especially useful when dealing with your children. Here is how it works.

You ask the executive a question and then stop talking. Count four seconds to yourself before you utter another sound. "1... 2... 3...4..." Before you get to four, the executive will start talking and answer your question. At that point you let her talk and keep talking. **Don't interrupt.** It is amazing how it works. She will start talking very slowly; as she thinks of more, she'll start speaking faster and faster. Then she will start to slow down and stop. At this point you say, "Uh-huh" or nod and count four seconds again without making a sound. "1...2...3...4..." She will start up again and take you along. After that you can do another Uh-huh; if it seem she has more, or you can move on to something else. Caution: It has to be a full 4 seconds – not 1,2,3,4. Now if the executive doesn't answer after four seconds, then jump in and either rephrase the question or ask if there is a problem with what you asked.

The four seconds is crucial. Bob Miller and Steve Heiman did research showing that the average time a person waits after asking a question is three-quarters to one and a half seconds. The questioner rephrases it, makes an additional comment, asks another question, or answers the question himself. In other words, he gives the executive no time to answer the question. It is tough to learn much about the individual or situation under these conditions.

The reason golden silence works is that people need time to formulate the answer, especially if it is a thought provoking question – something they are not use to getting. Once they get it sorted in their head, it starts flowing; and as they are talking, more things come into their head and are queuing up to come out. This is why their speech pattern quickens. Once they stop, they inevitably think of more. That's why you want to encourage them to go on with your, "Uh-huh."

I think of the conscious mind as a capacitor – a device to store electrical energy. As ideas are discharged from the capacitor, new ideas from the deeper mind fill it. Your silence has triggered the deeper mind to get all the information and associated ideas up to the surface. So this takes a few seconds, but once it gets going, the conscious mind and mouth can only go so fast. This is why you have to let them go. It is also analogous to fishing for big game fish or smaller fish with light tackle. Once the fish is hooked, you let it run. This is when the fish has the most power. If you try to stop it, the line will break and the communication will be cut off. Therefore, **never interrupt** once the executive starts talking. Don't interrupt even if they say they want to buy or commit. Let them finish the thought. Smile and keep nodding. Don't interrupt even if they say wonderful things about your competition or terrible things about you and/or your company. Let them finish the thoughts and get it all out of his or her system.

The power or this technique is multi-faceted. The biggest power-factor is that people like to listen to themselves a lot more than they like listening to you. They just need an opportunity. They will tell you their whole train of thought and how what you are selling relates to them. They know who you are and who you represent and what you want. They will tell you exactly how you can fit in – if you let them. This is what you want – instructions. It doesn't matter what you think they should want. Their wants (not yours) will be satisfied by you or someone else.

If you let them go, they will tell you much more than the question you asked. If you're prepared, as we said before, you will hook onto all this valuable information. You won't have to play 20 questions, which is self-serving and annoying.

When people get the whole charge out of their system, first they feel good; second, they usually are open to hear suggestions. They've gone as far as they can go and think you understand. It's like a session with a psychologist. He asks a few questions. You do all the talking and feel better. Then he gives some suggestions to change. The discharge process is necessary before you are able to accept new ideas or suggestions. This mental discharge also helps the executive organize her thoughts and create new thoughts. In some cases the executive may even determine the solution and tell you explicitly what you have to do. It is a very powerful technique.

Active Listening

Active listening means participating, without interrupting or disturbing the executive's train of thought, while she or he is talking. Be engaged. The best way I've found is by taking notes. As the executive is speaking, take notes. Some people feel it's rude. I feel it is rude not to. It shows that what this person is saying is important to you.

You want to capture what the executive is saying because she is telling you what you have to know and possibly do to establish a relationship with her. Everything she says is important to her. In addition she will say words that have meaning to her, and her meaning may be different than yours. These are what I call *power words,* and you want to capture these words without interruption. You'll go back to them later for clarification. For example, she may say I want a company that's dependable. Now your mind may have a vision of what dependable means, but it may be different than hers. Worse yet, she may not have consciously spelled out what dependable means to her. There are many words and concepts like this – reliability, good customer service, just-in-time, higher productivity, reduced costs, etc. You have to explore these further so that you both are clear on her meaning. Otherwise, you could both be very disappointed. You thought you "came through," and she thinks you didn't.

So as any of these words or concepts that you feel are potent come up – even if you feel you have a good understanding of the meaning – write them down and underline them. Don't interrupt. After she's finished releasing all the mental energy, mention that you'd like some clarification on a few of her words. "You said you'd like better customer service. What does good customer service look like to you?" Golden Silence – 1... 2... 3... 4.... She will now go off and start designing it or tell you exactly her vision. You will be amazed how clear they are and how much you'll learn.

Another duty while you're taking notes is to realize that as this executive is giving her vision, issues, etc., she will mention some feature or product you have that will address it to the tee. **Don't interrupt.** Even though you want to jump out of your seat, let her keep talking. Write your feature or product in the margin next to the notes for that moment. You don't want to lose this connection, but you don't want to bring it up now. Why? Because she will give you more good stuff if you let her talk. If you interrupt, she stops talking and the discharge is not complete. Additionally, if she stimulates ideas or questions in your head while she's talking, don't interrupt. Write down the idea or question and circle it. You can explore it or ask a question later.

Don't Interview at Meals

Since we don't want interruptions when your executive is spilling reams of critical information, don't start your interview at lunch or dinner. Think what happens. You sit down and get comfortable – maybe order a drink. You ask your first question – Golden Silence 1... 2.... 3. He thinks. Starts answering – slowly then speeding up. It's getting good. You're taking notes, underlining, making notes in the margin. All of a sudden you hear, "Are you ready to order?" Both of you mumble and say something to the server. The thoughts are lost. The moment is shattered. You try to reestablish the moment only to get interrupted again, and again, and again.

Meals are a terrible place to conduct meaningful interviews. An alternative is to meet at an office around 10:30 and do the interview. Then go to lunch. Save a personal or sensitive topic for lunch, remembering you will be interrupted. Otherwise, save the discussion for coffee – less interruptions. You can also mention to the server that you will call her when you're ready to order. This may appear pushy or controlling to the hungry executive – as he stuffs bread into his mouth.

I prefer 10:30 a.m. because if you practice Golden Silence, and clear up power words, this will easily take 1½ hours. The executive won't even care because she is doing the talking. You will both feel as if it were 10 minutes. If you do the meeting at 11:00 a.m., it's 11:15 by the time the admin picks you up, 11:30 to do pleasantries and ask your first question. Then the exec will want to leave by 11:45 to beat the lunch crowd and get a table. This doesn't leave much time. It's better to start earlier.

If it's a dinner thing, do cocktails – away from the TV. Did you ever notice how much good conversation takes place in a car? There are no interruptions.

Confirm the Discussion

Steven Covey, in his *7 Habits of Highly Effective People*, says you have to listen with an ear for understanding. Again, what the executive is saying may not mean the same to you as it does to her. Therefore, you have to clear up any ambiguities and confirm that you both understand what her words mean. If she knows you understand, you now have a pass to get back to her.

This is your responsibility alone because your executive feels he has given all the information and unless you ask more questions you've got it. You may think you've got it, but you must be certain. This is what you are basing your presentation on. This is what you are using to establish the relationship on. Therefore you want to get confirmation that your understanding is correct. You might say something like this, "Just to be sure I understand everything you've said, let me give it back to you. You said you wanted.... Is this correct?" This will usually get the executive going for another 10 minutes. Keep writing and learning. This helps the executive clarify his thinking which is good for you. You are now consulting even though you've given nothing. However the executive is realizing what he knows and what he doesn't know. He will now be open to suggestions, ideas, and new concepts.

What's really wonderful about Golden Silence, Active Listening, and Confirming is that they take all the pressure off you. The executive will do the talking and love it. You will get all the information necessary for you to make a targeted presentation and she will want to hear what you have to offer. She feels you understand. You have earned credibility by asking about her, listening to what she's saying, clarifying for understanding, and confirming that you understand.

CHAPTER **20**

Learn Their
Personality Style
and Create Great Chemistry

Executives, as with others, are different. They have different interests and different styles. They interact with people differently and relate to what people say or do differently. To establish a relationship or just be involved with an executive, it is important to understand his personality type. You must appeal to his style or it will be as though you are speaking a foreign language. Take notice of people you get along with. They are either the same types as you or you have learned how to appeal to their type. Friction usually occurs when there is a conflict of style. The way you approach an issue or solution is different than the other person. Unfortunately you lose credibility in this person's eyes even though you are dead-on correct. Therefore, to get anywhere (to ask questions or to present or to establish a relationship) you have to be sensitive to the executive's personality type and adapt to how he likes to work with people.

There is an excellent program that I teach called Social Styles by Wilson Learning. It is all about people interactions in organizations. There is also a program called the Versatile salesperson, which is Social Styles structured for salespeople interacting with customers. They both cover the same topic of personal interaction. Meyers Briggs is also popular. There are two books – *Collaborative Selling*, by Tony Alexandra, and *Reading People* by Jo-Ellan Dimities. I will not go into depth on this, but here is a quick overview.

Basically people are broken into four personality types. These are broken down further into sub-types. I'll leave the derivation of how this happens to the books or programs. The four types are Driver, Analytical, Expressive, and Amiable (using the Wilson Learning version).

Drivers, as the name implies, want to make things happen. They are forceful, in a hurry, get to the point kinds of people. A driver might say, "Tell me what you've got. I'm in a hurry. What will it do for me? You've got 10 minutes."

Analyticals are very detail oriented. They want all the information in logical, descriptive, graphical, chart form. They want to see the research reports, the success stories, the percentages, the lists, etc. An analytical might say, "I need more data. Let's calculate the total investment and returns. Where is the research to support this? Let's go see some installations."

Expressives are the party types. They want to get everybody together to discuss it, play with it, ask questions, see it. They strike up conversations with everyone to get consensus and have a good time. An expressive might say, "Let's get Tom, Mary, and Jane in here to talk about it. In the meantime let me tell you about all the fun stuff going on around here. Let's get a golf outing together with lots of your people and lots of ours."

Amiables are very friendly, nurturing people. They invite you in to talk about your product/service in a very friendly way. They want to take you under their wing, listen to you and make you feel very warm and welcome. An amiable might say, "Let's get a cup of coffee. Sit here. This is a nice place to talk. Now, tell me all about yourself, your company, and your products."

Now people have a sub-type of the same four styles. For example, I am an analytical-driver. "Give me all the charts and support information – fast." "How soon can we make a site tour?" My daughter is an expressive-amiable. "Let's get everybody together, but be sure they all get a personal invitation and understand the reason for the meeting." She will then greet each one personally and make them feel very comfortable. My wife is an expressive-driver. "Let's go to that outing, but we've got to come back with four resumes, two commitments, and a job offer." An associate in my office complex is an amiable-analytical. He comes into my office, makes sure he's not interrupting, and gets into the details of what I'm doing. When I ask about his business, I get chapter and verse, percentages, time tables, and prescribed medication.

He and I have conflicting personalities – amiable and driver. When you mix conflicting personalities, there is a good chance of conflict. If I'm busy and not interested in the topic de jour, I can be rude – driver. Yet he's such a nice guy – amiable, that I have to watch myself so as not to hurt his feelings. To complicate things further, people will have a style that may be the same or different under stress. So if you catch an amiable in a hurry or with a lot going on around him, another style might surface.

As mentioned above, to be successful, you will have to determine what type of personality this executive you're interviewing has. In order to ask questions and more importantly to present your information, you will have to adapt to his style to make him feel comfortable with you. With me you will have to give me the key points up front and support them with facts – fast. With my daughter you will have to bring people from your or her organization and have a friendly lunch where everybody mingles to discuss the plans. With my wife you will have to bring your staff and deliver results. She will not care how you get them, just as long as everybody agrees. With my office associate, plan on a one-on-one lunch with brochures and details. Do not expect a decision. This will take time.

Now there are all kinds of combinations, especially when you add stress to the equation. So to make it easy on yourself, just observe how this person is interacting with you. What two styles do you see? If you are practicing Golden Silence you'll have plenty of time to observe. If you're talking, you have to observe and talk at the same time. This is difficult because you'll be under stress. Although many people do this, it can be very misleading. You may think you're connecting, yet this is an amiable who doesn't want to hurt your feelings. You may think you've scored big by getting someone to listen to you, yet it is an expressive who is not going to sit through this alone. You may think you lost the interest of the executive, yet it is a driver needing to move to the next mountain. Therefore, listening and observing is far more accurate. You might even ask the executive what manner of interview/presentation he would prefer.

You can also draw generalities about people from their functional position. CEOs might be drivers. Sales and marketing executives might be expressives. Human Resources people might be amiables. Engineers and IT people might be analyticals. But be careful. The second type and the stress factors affect this. Once again, you'll be able to assess the type better as you listen and observe under different conditions.

Workshop

Select an executive. Where do you stand on the credibility pyramid? What will you do to move up or how did you fail on the last step? What do you want to know about this executive? What questions will you ask? What is the personality style?

Section V

Forming
the Relationship

CHAPTER 21

Ingratiate the Executive
by Using Your Arsenal of Information

Now that you've overcome the obstacles of getting to your executive, and now that you've interviewed and listened to him, you should have a good idea of what's important to him and his style. Therefore you are now in a position to present how you can provide what he values and present it in a style that's comfortable for him to listen to.

Make no mistake this executive wants to **only** hear about what can help him. It is the time to address all the issues, problems, desires, and interests he's told you about. Stray from this and you lose him. However, you will have to remind him of what he said because he may have forgotten what he told you.

For example, suppose the executive said that his salespeople are reluctant to call on executives. Don't just start presenting the trinity as a tool to build confidence and overcome executive fear. Rather, confirm with him that this is still a problem. Use the confirmation as a reminder before you present. "You mentioned your salespeople are reluctant to call on senior executives." Look for a nod or ask, "Is this correct?" If yes, then move forward to the trinity concept, how to implement it with salespeople and managers, and how others have benefited.

The reasoning here is to keep showing the executive that you are focused on what he has said. By confirming these issue, it shows your focus is on him. It offers an opportunity to see if his interest has changed or been satisfied already. It also offers the opportunity for him to get back to the pain he felt when he told you, so he will appreciate your offering when you present. Finally, it offers the opportunity for him to contribute more information about this issue and/or other issues on his mind. The more issues and suggestions he offers you, the more ammunition you have for your targeted presentation. The more he tells you, the more you will know his style and how he wants to be sold.

The Value Proposition

The only value proposition for this executive is what he values. However, you have been conditioned by your marketing department and your role models to present your value proposition. You use product catalogues, glossy brochures, and your knowledge of the competition to tell people why they should buy what you think should be important to them, and that they should buy it from you. You should have been conditioned to determine what's valuable to this executive. This is his value proposition and the only one that counts. Your job is to address this better than the competition.

This is a meaningful shift and it will be tough to accept because of your conditioning. For an adult, old habits are tough to break. As discussed before, you've been conditioned to present. You've learned (incorrectly) that your value proposition is what your company has to offer that can solve a problem which most customers in this industry face. You even know how to position this value proposition positively against the competition.

What you're missing, however, is the executive's vision and his value package. Even if he faces this general problem, your competitors have or will position themselves in the same way you've been conditioned to do it. Then you both look alike to the executive and there is no reason to have a relationship with either of you. He'll go out for bids the next time he needs your product/service and select the lowest price.

Therefore, you must prepare your value package based on the executive's vision. This is not the time to try to change it. This should have been done in your consulting phase when you were interviewing with him. Once his vision is established, he's not going to want to change it. The more you try, the more you look controlling and seem annoying. Who wants a relationship with a controlling, annoying person?

It's About Results, Not Product

This executive will form a relationship with you if he can see you as a resource to help him with his career. Product benefits and features are what his people enjoy and use. These are expected and must be in place. However, what he wants for himself are those results that will advance him or that will get him out of trouble with minimum risk of failure or loss. This is the kind of information he will give you during the interview if you ask him questions about himself and listen to what he says.

Your mission is to grasp and learn these non-product/service issues. You must be alert to hear the issue, if raised, and prepared to ask leading questions if it doesn't come out. For example, there is nothing wrong in telling this individual that you want to be considered a valuable asset to him and then ask him, "What will it take to be considered an asset to you?" You then must determine how to show him he can obtain this from you. This may be difficult because these are soft issues that usually can't be guaranteed – i.e. make him look good to the CEO or Board, help him take advantage of situations or overcome obstacles or advance his vision for the future. It will require strategizing. How you will do it? How can he believe he will make headway through you? As we'll discuss later, it may take implementation and time in service. However, without your connecting his vision to your offering, you'll be lucky if he recognizes your value by himself. Luck is not what I'd want to base my success on.

Presenting the Value Proposition

Based on the discussion above, the executive's vision is *the* value proposition that counts, not your vision or your value proposition. I'm using "the" because it changes from executive to executive.

Your competitors are trying to position themselves to look better than you. You are trying to position yourself to look better than the competitors. All of you are usually beating each other up one way or another instead of focusing in on the executive. Let's assume, however, that you have done your interviewing and that you know what the executive values. Your next challenge is to present to him in a way that the competitors can't come behind you and say, "We have that, too."

This is called differentiation. Nothing new, but what's difficult is how you do it. It could be that the difference is slight, and it's not in your favor. It could be you don't know if there is a difference: "We have that and so do they." The best way to deal with this differentiation issue is to *quantify* what you have. This means describing with numbers, in detail, what you *do* have. You cannot present in general terms. As an example, the customer says he would like good service. From your interviewing you know what good service looks like to him. So now you *cannot* say that you have excellent service. Why? – because your competitors can come from behind and say the same thing. You say, for example, "We have excellent service. Our people are well trained."

"Our people are well trained," says the competitor, and so on.

What you have to describe is that you have 24-hour, 7-day service using 13 regional service offices in 27 cities staffed with 82 people who have been through a minimum of 400 hours of training and apprenticeship. We guarantee a response to your call within 6 minutes. We have 7 regional warehouses with at least 2,000 square feet of spare parts. We guarantee shipment to your facility within 24 hours. We have a fleet of 54 vans stocked with 400 of the most frequently used spare parts, etc.

Your competitors cannot say that. Typically they won't say anything like this. They will probably just say, "We have excellent service." They may even show a brochure with pictures of vans and pretty ladies and men with headsets and toolboxes. They can't say, "We have that, too," because (1) they don't, and (2) the customer will not explain how detailed you were so they won't go into detail. And even if they do, their details may not match yours.

So the customer is left with the impression of what you have detailed – probably a good picture. The competitor's pictures are fuzz. Your quantification will leave a formidable impression on this executive. It shows you're prepared, you're thorough, and that you understand his vision.

The caution is that you cannot wing this.

(1) You have to know what's important to the executive and confirm it. Otherwise you will bore him to death with details and he'll get rid of you. If you're on target, he will listen intently and ask questions.

(2) It should be customized for this executive so that details merge and support many of his vision items. Otherwise, you'll sound like a response to a spec sheet. We all know that executives don't read those because they are boring and cover lots of stuff they're not interested in. That's why there are executive summaries – which are also terrible. There should be an executive summary for one executive and another for another, with each detailing your proposal for each executive's vision.

(3) Pay attention to the smaller details. This may be your differentiation. Your competitors will all address the big issues. The better interviewer will have learned all personal components and the details, as well as the main party line issues as described in the general specification or bid document.

CHAPTER 22

Deliver the Expectations
and Win the Executive

Selling the first order or a few subsequent orders doesn't mean you have a relationship with the executive. Sure she trusts you and you've moved up the credibility pyramid, but now you have to deliver – and not just the product/service but the results. Delivering the results is going to require the resources of your company. You are the connection between the buyer and the supplier. You are the information link. You are the coordinator. You are the mediator. Will your company configure it correctly, build it properly, deliver it on time, and service it satisfactorily? These are functions you cannot control, but you can keep track of what is happening. When problems arise, you will have to address them and keep everybody informed. Problems will come from different places and everyone will blame each other, including your company people, your customer, and you. You have got to be the one who stops the chain of blame and moves everyone toward solutions.

The key is to keep the executive informed. You should discuss up front how she wants to be kept informed. Some executives like all the grizzly details. Other will want progress reports. Still others only want to know when it's been resolved – "no excuses, just results." Sometimes the executive's subordinate or even the executive is to blame. In cases like this you must be sensitive yet you must also be open, honest, and upfront. Explain the situation. Ask how she perceives it. Explain how you and your company perceive it. Ask for and discuss possible solutions. Getting someone to accept blame isn't necessary. You could be *dead right*, but it will not change the circumstances. The other party could be *dead right* and it won't change the circumstances. Each could see oneself as right and guess what – you are still where you are. So focus on a solution rather than placement of blame.

I recently had an issue with an airline. I wanted to purchase a ticket over the phone. The service person took all of the information. I asked for an e-ticket and asked, "Please fax me the itinerary and a receipt." Well I got the itinerary, but no receipt, so I called. The new service person told me that they issued me a paper ticket. I politely told her that I wanted an e-ticket.

This was important because I forgot a paper ticket once and it was a nightmare. I couldn't get on the flight because it was booked, even though I was one of the booked people. Others were ahead of me on the wait list. To make it worse I had to get on another flight at full fare. This made me a believer of e-tickets.

So the service person tells me it is too late. I'm getting a paper ticket. I ask why didn't I get an e-ticket – and by now I'm talking to the supervisor. She tells me that I used Sam for the ticket and Samuel for the credit card. Shocked again, I explained that I didn't know, and I didn't do it intentionally, and why is it such a problem. Had the first service person explained it, I would have gladly changed the ticket to Samuel. "Too late, you're getting a paper ticket." Well it degenerated from here to the point where I said, "Forget it. I will return the ticket and fly another airline."

Now either the service person or the supervisor could have said, "Well Sam or Samuel, we have a situation. What kind of solution can we work out together – *realizing we both have constraints.*" What does it matter who's to blame? What does matter is what can we do now.

The reason this gets testy is because of egos and fear of loss. Accepting blame is ego deflating or raises fear of the ramifications it will have. I might have to do more work or my boss will feel I couldn't handle the situation. Getting the other to accept blame is ego building and eliminates the fear of loss. Few people like to get their egos deflated or accept losses – even if they believe they're wrong. It's hard. They may be angry that they're in this awkward or hostile situation. So when you see problems coming, move away from egos; address losses and move toward possible solutions. If the other person is unrelenting in trying to blame, just nod and keep pushing toward solution. "I'm sorry you feel that way. I'm not sure what happened ... but what can we do *together*?" Always get the word "together" in the solution. Sooner or later they will get the message that you are trying to solve the problem and then they will become part of the solution.

Implementation In-Process

As the implementation progresses and is completed, you now have to monitor whether the results are being met. Many salespeople will follow up after a short time and ask how things are going. The responses will vary all over the map depending on the moment and depending on whom you ask. What you get may not be indicative of what's really happening, or more importantly, of whether the results are actually being met.

Therefore, you have to frame your questions to focus on what you are looking for. What specifically did this executive tell you that she wanted your products or services to do? You might say, "You told me you wanted ... Are you getting it?" "How has it affected you personally?"

Ask the subordinate people these questions *before* you approach the executives. You may be able to correct some things or use some success stories when you speak with the executive. However, success for subordinates may not be success for the executive. Success to her is her focus.

Measurements

There will always be ambiguities about performance because perceptions of expectations are different. That's why you need to take time to define them and establish a way to measure results. Pat Riley, the successful coach of professional basketball (Lakers, Knicks, and Miami Heat) tells in his book how he measures every aspect of his players' performances – their court time, shots taken, percentages, distance of shot, speed, etc. However, he is measuring it for his own application. He draws correlation to success and then uses those statistics for future decisions. In like manner your executive is measuring your performance against his standards. He may not be doing it consciously or analytically, but he is measuring the results against his expectations. He then uses that measurement for future decisions. "Did these results meet my expectations and help me advance my situation?" "Do I want to use this person and company again?"

Therefore you have to develop a measurement system to gauge your progress. What to measure is what the executive will have to tell you. You may be thinking ease of implementation. He's thinking time to market. So be sure you are measuring what's important to him.

These measurements will show that either you have to correct them or that you can use them to your advantage. The part about correcting is obvious. However, using them to your advantage is something you have to do. If you have successfully met the measurements you must show or remind the executive that you delivered. You must become associated with the successful results. Executives may not notice when things go well because they are so focused on what's not working. Another reason is that no one keeps score. There is no celebration in the end zone and no points shown on the scoreboard. That's why you have to point out the results and become associated with the success. Executives forget. Executives associate the results with others or themselves. These and other reasons are why you must promote your involvement and receive recognition. Without this your chances of a relationship or further business is going to be like the first sale – tough.

The results that matter and the measurements that count are the ones this particular executive has established with you. Your perception of what should be important doesn't matter. Nor does your measurement system. What also counts is how the others in his organization measure your offering against their expectations. If you want positive relationships with subordinates and other executives, you will have to understand their methods of measurement. However, to keep it manageable, be sure everyone knows the others' measurements. Be particularly vocal about the metrics and expectations for the executive you are focusing on. Share the others' measurements with him. Your metrics have to focus on each executive that you want a relationship with.

Everything can be Measured

Many times you'll be faced with an individual who just gives you some arbitrary guidelines of what's expected. When making a sale there may be very complete specifications on the make-up of the product. The expected results are usually less specific. People want it better, but what does 'better' mean and who's defining this? You show or prove in some way to a purchasing agent that you have all the nitty-gritty requirements and that he's OK – and you move forward. Those who use your products or services sense the benefit and you move forward. Similarly, executives have to move forward before you move forward. Unless they connect you to that success, you won't establish a relationship. Much of the time the executive will credit oneself for the success. "It was me who had the foresight to use your company."

People will say that they want better performance. They want better service. They want better reliability. As we discussed before, we need to question these people to learn what these words mean to them. If you keep drilling, this can be defined to a very specific, quantitative level.

A customer recently said to me, "I want my salespeople to be perceived by the brokers as more professional, and I want my senior managers to see my salespeople as more professional." As I persisted with questions – "What makes you feel that your salespeople are not seen that way?" and "How does a professional salesperson look to you?" – I started to realize that it was all about getting the brokers to introduce these salespeople to the end customer. We then decided that our measurement system would be the number of times a broker brings the salesperson to the customer. We then developed a way to track it without doing another report. This customer also wanted more sales – easy to measure. Wrong. Increased sales can come from many methods. So we had to define how we would measure my impact. This happened by defining behaviors that make a salesperson successful. We then measured if the salesperson was behaving accordingly. How often was something happening and to what degree of success? We are now correlating this to his sales dollars.

Sometimes new reports are necessary. Don't add reports to an already full load. If you are going to add, you have to eliminate. Reports were established to measure criteria and link it to another success criteria – such as, "If you make more sales calls, you'll make more sales and more sales are good for profitability." Not necessarily true, but it was a system built for a particular time by particular people. Well, times change as do people. But somehow reports remain. Therefore either you have to merge or extract your measurement into or from an existing report or replace that report with something for the times and the executive in charge.

As you can imagine, these measurements and reports are not discussions that come easily when you are trying to make a sale or negotiate terms. There are two very appropriate times when you'll get maximum attention, information, and enhanced credibility. The first is on your initial meeting. People know they have to inform you of what they want to buy and they will be open to give you all sorts of information about the results, themselves, or their world. The other time is just after you've made the sale. You want to do a great job for these people. To do it you need to learn what each expects and how each will measure it. This is the best time to get introduced to all the executives. They will be very open to see you and define their success factors and metrics. Once again, you have not been conditioned to do this. How do you feel about getting a lot of personal information on the first visit? – Probably uncomfortable, afraid, and/or nervous. How often do you go in after a sale to meet all of the high level executives that you haven't met and have implementation discussions with all direct and indirect executives?

The most important thing for you is having the focus to do this. On first engagements, most salespeople *present* what their company does rather than learn what results the customer wants and how she will know if she gets them. Then after they make the sale they forget this account and move onto some other opportunity. Successful salespeople realize more opportunities come from satisfied executives and it is easy money. New accounts are tough money.

The final elements about measuring are your benchmarks. You need to know your starting position or metric and you need to have a system. The starting position is obvious but often not easy. Many times your executive has not been measuring what he has and now you have to show that it has gotten better. This will require a little work on both your parts to establish what exists. The other benchmark is what must be done to produce the result. Computers are beautiful because if you do it right it works, if you don't it doesn't. It's frustrating, but reliable. Life is not that way. Therefore, you have to establish ground rules that, if followed, should produce the results.

This is not meant to be your out, but the executive should understand that she has responsibilities, too. If this discussion doesn't happen you can't go back later and tell her she should have known. As an extreme example, I refinanced my house. I signed at least 45 documents stating every conceivable condition that could exist so that I could not go back and say, "I didn't know that." We made it more interesting by the agent telling a short story of how someone sued or was exonerated from not paying the mortgage payment because he or she didn't know something. Now you don't have to do this, but your executive has to know and sign up to her responsibility. There is no way I can improve a sales team's performance without the support of managers reinforcing the concepts with the salespeople. These are the system benchmarks. However, I shouldn't wait until my system fails to go back and tell her. I want it to succeed, so I have regular conversations about what's working and what's not. If I don't hear anything, that's bad.

Using the Results

As already noted here, the results you measure have to be in a measure that your executive relates to and agrees to. You then have the responsibility to deliver your product/service and monitor the results accordingly. If you are working with multiple executives and they are looking for different kinds of results, you will have to monitor multiple results. This is not uncommon. In the example above the VP of Sales wanted sales increases. The Director of Broker Relations wanted more meetings with brokers.

With metrics you can evaluate the results. If the metrics are showing positive results, you then present them to your executive. Ask her how she *feels* about these results. Sit back and listen. Notice I didn't say think. I said feel. Thinking is done in the head. Feeling is done in the gut. Decisions and relationships are developed in the gut and justified in the head.

Now if she doesn't feel good about the results and/or your metrics are not so good, then you've got to implement a correction/improvement plan. Get with your management, your operations, your service people, etc., to discuss what can be done to improve the results. Talk to your executive's subordinates to get ideas from them. You should also be discussing this with your executive. Share your team's ideas to correct or improve the situation and ask for her ideas. There will be no future business or relationship with this executive unless her results are met. You have the responsibility (not your team) to pull it together if you want the relationship.

When I was selling high tech material handling systems, I sold a very big system to Hewlett Packard. It was a new printer project and they had plans for many more projects. The concept took a lot to sell, but it finally happened. My company installed the system. It worked great except that the motors on these little cars kept burning out. My company blamed the users. HP said they weren't powerful enough. My company was busy with other projects and engineering didn't want to design a new motor, housing, etc. However, I was thinking about all this future business that was about to go south if this didn't get corrected without a bad taste in the executives' mouths. It was my job, therefore, to get this corrected. I could not pass the blame or the responsibility. This is where I learned that establishing relationships internally was just as important as establishing them externally. You, as the salesperson or sales manager, are obliged to give the parties a Win-Win. If you do, you also win. If you don't give them the Win-Win or they get it without you, you lose. So it's in your best interest to take responsibility even if someone else is appointed to deal with this. In your mind, and through your demeanor, you are in charge.

Now if your executive feels good about the results, then capture that feeling in a confirmation. It could be a statement such as, "That's great. Then you agree that my company and I have met your expectations." You can also ask her to sign a letter that you've drafted stating the results and the metrics and her feelings. You want to use it as a testimonial but you need her permission. If she doesn't want it public information, then you just want to show your management and keep for your own records.

This is the point when your relationship starts. This executive has felt a benefit from your efforts. It is now up to you to leverage this relationship and to develop a plan to maintain it.

You work or leverage this relationship by getting the opportunity for more business ahead of the competition. You leverage it by getting information to help you get more business. You leverage it by getting introductions and meetings with other key executives in the organization. You leverage it by getting referrals to others you feel could use your services. This is your reward for providing personal professional impact (PPI) to this executive. In other words, you enter her into your Golden Network.

So you ask her what other business you can start working on or expect to get from her. If there is none on the near horizon, then ask if she will set up a meeting for you to assess the other executives' feelings. The intent is to build credibility and start a relationship with these other executives. Start working on getting them into your Golden Network. You never know what changes will be occurring in the near future. Conditions change, people move, and positive professional relationships are immune to times and conditions.

Workshop

Use the worksheet below to address how you will implement and measure results. Then address how you will either make improvements or leverage the relationship.

Establishing Relationship Worksheet

What Questions Will You Ask to Uncover Executive's Feelings about Implementation?

How Will You Show You Delivered Results that Met His/Her Expectations and Measurements?

Do You Have Plans for Improvements? (If Necessary)

What Additional Business Can You Discuss?
(Is it Appropriate?)

1. _____

2. _____

3. _____

Section VI

Maintaining
the Relationship

CHAPTER 23

Positive Professional Impacts
Bond the Relationship

Delivering the results to the executive in the manner and quantity she wanted will be the beginning of the relationship. By doing this, the executive then attains what's inherently important to her success. She has done her job, maybe taken care of some doubters, maybe put herself in a position for a promotion or a raise in salary/bonus/commission, maybe gained some self satisfaction, maybe relieved some stress, managed to keep her job, etc. This is what matters to her and she gets it from the business results you delivered. These are examples of positive professional impacts.

Your role is to have an impact on the results so that she can benefit professionally. Then the relationship will be established. Before that, you are still at the "getting to know her" stage. No matter how social and friendly your interactions, you are in the courting stage until you deliver results that she values and benefits professionally from. There will be no relationship until then.

This is what relationships are all about – each person getting something from the other so that both win. She gets the satisfactory results that she's required to deliver and thus gets her personal, professional win from her company managers. You get some orders, the results you are responsible for, and you get your personal, professional win from your company managers. Notice the emphasis on the word professional. Executive relationships are professional. They may lead to social, but social is not necessary nor does it have any strength to withstand adversity or challenge.

The Myth of Social Relationships

Let's explore this often mistaken concept of building a social relationship. Many people believe that good salespeople are born. They believe that they have a gregarious nature, can socialize and that people like them. With these qualities they will be able to establish a relationship and people will buy from them. These qualities may get them in the door – and getting in the door is extremely important. However, it will not keep the door open unless they deliver what this executive wants and they will not get the chance to deliver until there is trust and believability. Therefore, getting in the door is not enough.

What these gregarious people exude is confidence and/or comfort in dealing with people. Each is probably an expressive or amiable type personality. These individuals are great at a party meeting people or are just so nice you've got to love them. They've done it all their lives and they feel comfortable doing it.

What they have to learn is what to do after they get in the door to keep the door open. They have to hone their professional skills to obtain the necessary information and get it to others. They have to learn what the bottom line results are and how to deliver them. Many of my clients complain that their salespeople have all of these great relationships with low level people and spend considerable time with them, but their sales are terrible. These gregarious yet poor salespeople need to focus on the professional aspects, which people are *not* born with. An example would be a great carpenter. This person can saw, measure, and assemble wood beautifully. But ask that person to build a house or a bridge or a piece of furniture and it will be a challenge because he or she doesn't know about design loads, stresses, tolerances, or precision. These are learned skills.

Other types of people, such as analytical and dominant personalities, may struggle with socializing. That doesn't make them less of a salesperson. Actually they may be better because once they do get to the executives and get the executive comfortable with them, they focus on what has to be done to deliver results. These people need to learn how to approach prospects and interview them without being pushy or boring.

Another misconception is that executives want social things – bagels, donuts, tickets for sporting events, lunches, dinners, fishing trips, etc. The professionals who really count want results first. Their jobs and their careers are far more important to them than your friendship or your token gifts. Unless specifically asked for, gifts are things that *you* like. You may be assuming the executive also likes them. Think about Christmas or birthday gifts. You get some real random stuff because the giver feels that she would like it, therefore, you will like it. The buyers who specifically ask for gifts should immediately raise a big stop sign in your head.

CHAPTER **24**

Stay Involved
or Your Competitor Will
Steal Your Relationship

Relationships are based on both parties winning. As already mentioned, a party wins when she receives a positive professional impact from the results delivered. You deliver bagels, the people smile and thank you and you hope there will be a payback to keep you involved with them. Notice how many people stay around to help you after you deliver the bagels. Executives and professionals don't have time for bagels or are watching their weight. They don't have time for lunches, dinners, golf, or fishing trips either. You're hoping that by dangling this bait, you'll get a bite of her attention. Moral to the story – learn what she's biting on. It will always be what can solve her professional problems, not her social calendar.

On the other hand, if you keep giving gifts or results to someone who does have the time and you still don't get anything, how eager are you to continue giving? Many salespeople fall into the fear column with this. They fear that if they don't give, they won't get anything. If this is the case, try giving a few times. See what happens. If you get nothing or less than what you want, then it's time to cut him loose and move on. The good salespeople work on providing the professional results and getting orders. Their thoughts and actions are focused on the professional aspects. Once the customer gives them what they want – the order or whatever – these salespeople then give social gifts as a thank you. They don't give before as a bribe. Many salespeople give no gifts, because it's not necessary. If you paid for these gifts yourself, how often and to whom would you give them? The best gifts are the professional results. If you both get your professional results, you will have a strong relationship.

Results make for a relationship. As you move forward with this executive, continuing to deliver results will keep the relationships alive. As results go, so goes the relationship. However, expected results are dynamic. Conditions and times change, producing different problems and opportunities which require different solutions – different results. Even if conditions didn't change, people get used to what was given and the impact weakens. As this happens, your relationship weakens. Remember a project or sale you worked on and how close you got to someone as you interviewed, presented and implemented. You were tight. After a while, you were off doing other sales and you lost track of this individual. Then you decide to call and you find the person busy, aloof, or polite at best. Your relationship has weakened because you haven't done anything for him lately.

Therefore, to maintain a relationship you must continue to provide positive professional impact. To do this you must keep current with this executive and his business. Through frequent discussions, keep current with the challenges of his job. Learn about his company by keeping current with reports and publications – Annual Reports, 10K's, 10Q's, articles, trade journals, the company website. Talk to the executive's subordinates and associates about the company, their jobs, and challenges. Learn about the industry and changing conditions with customers, with competition, and the way they go to market. Check out trade associations, trade publications, trade shows, and general economic and professional news. This information will keep you close to the changing conditions. You'll be able to offer ideas or other services (results) you can provide to help. Finally, stay current with the executive's perception of your capabilities. As times change and as your competition continues to assault you, your capabilities may not come across as good as they once did. Again, "What have you done for me lately?" is what the executive is thinking. In your frequent discussions, offer up ideas that other companies you sell are doing or exploring. Be consultative. Don't push products. Bring articles or white papers. Take him on field trips to other companies or installations. Most importantly, help this executive do what he wants to do, better.

CHAPTER 25

Build a Plan to Maintain the Relationship

A strong, positive, professional relationship is an asset and should be managed as one. Think of something of value that you've worked hard to get – a car, a home, or a position in your company. All of these assets must be cared for and nurtured. Otherwise they will deteriorate and lose their value. Similarly, a professional relationship must be cared for and nurtured.

You care for your assets by investing in and maintaining them. You wash your car. You change the oil and tires and do routine maintenance. You clean your house. You paint it regularly and make repairs. You replace equipment as it breaks down – water heaters, dishwashers, etc. You may even make upgrades to serve you and increase the value. In your job you stay current with industry trends and competitive activities. You attend seminars and belong to associations. Similarly, you must make investments in your professional relationship.

Unlike an inanimate object, a real person is dynamic. This means your care and investment schedule is ever changing. Conditions are constantly changing in this executive's world. Some conditions are based on his environment, industry, or company, and some are self-imposed. Having a relationship with you is an expenditure on his part and must be rewarded. You have to continue to help this person as the conditions change. You must continue to give positive professional impacts.

Similarly, having a relationship with an executive is an expense to you and must be rewarded. As conditions in your environment, industry, company and/or yourself change, you will expect this executive to help you with the changes. If he doesn't the relationship will lose its punch, fade, deteriorate to eventually an acquaintance.

In a relationship both parties must benefit or else it's a dysfunctional one – and we all know that these lead to craziness. This happens often in business, and usually to the giving salesperson. The customer keeps asking for more and more and the salesperson keeps giving. An inordinate amount of time is used and there are few rewards, thus resulting in poor job performance. As with most dysfunctional relationships, the giver ends up down and out – wondering what happened. Therefore your professional relationship with an executive must provide benefits to both you as well as to the executive.

The benefits in a professional relationship must be based on corporate performance measurements. The executive will get personal wins as a result, but these wins are derived from the business, not you. As an example, by working with senior management and sales departments I help companies increase their sales. If the sales increase, the VP of Sales may get a promotion or some other reward. As conditions change or more sales are required, he will continue to use me. He has connected me to the performance improvements. I will get business from him, which gives me more income that allows me to buy things for my family or myself. As conditions change with me, or I need more business, I continue to use him for referrals, suggestions, and contracts. We both win through business. Therefore the business is the bond and it is a very powerful bond. As the business changes, your contribution to the business must change or the bond weakens.

In professional relationships the personal benefit comes indirectly. Someone other than you gives it to the executive. You affected the executive's performance that got him his promotion. Social relationships depend on the personal benefits. You have fun with someone and he has fun with you. You intellectually enjoy each other. You party well together. The personal benefit or feeling of happiness comes directly from the social interaction.

This is where lots of salespeople get confused. They believe that if they become very social with an executive, they will get more business. They do this because someone has told them that they must develop relationships with their buyers. Since they've never learned about professional relationships, they fall back on what they've seen and experienced in life – social relationships. They get friendly, they buy dinner, they buy gifts, and they take them on trips. This misguided salesperson then expects the executive to respect him and give him some business.

There are significant problems with this kind of thinking. These social relationships take a good deal of time and money to develop. They are tough because the executive is looking for business results, not a friend. These relationships are tenuous because the executive will end it as soon as professional results wane. Social relationships don't transfer well. When your social executive leaves, you won't have a basis to stay fixed in that company. Additionally, it is tough to develop relationships with other executives in the company based solely on a social relationship with another. However, if you are a contributor to business results, the others will easily see the value in your services and open the door for a relationship.

Professional relationships are business oriented with two dynamic parties who both benefit. Therefore, an interactive, mutually beneficial, ongoing business plan must be developed and worked in order to maintain your executive relationship.

Since it is mutually beneficial, both parties must participate. You do not prepare this plan alone. Your executive must participate. Expectations must be met for both and both must agree to make them happen for each. It must be built together with give and take on each side. It is interactive. Since it involves both of your companies, other members should participate and contribute from time to time. It must be action oriented, with responsibilities and deadlines assigned. It must be continuously monitored and updated. It should be reworked as conditions change and reviewed regularly to adjust for subtle changes.

This will assure the communication link, and as we all know, great relationships are built on good communication. A business plan for a relationship may sound a little formal, but if this relationship is important it should be formal. Think of marriage. How important is marriage and how formal is the paperwork? Remember this executive relationship is an asset and as such you must have a schedule for investments, maintenance, and assessment.

Build an Interactive, On-Going Business Plan
Background
There are many ways to build plans. My preference is to over-emphasize the do-it-together part and focus on expectations. History or background is good for a review and a reminder of past benefits. It goes to enhancing credibility. Write it down. It is also good as a benchmark of where you've been and where you are now. It can also serve as a gauge to how successful the relationship has been. In more operational language – where did you both expect to be and how does that compare to where you are?

The past is experience to glean from. Learn from the mistakes and duplicate the successes. Write it down.

Expectations
The next part of the plan is expectations. What do you both expect to accomplish with this relationship? What positive pro-

fessional impacts do you expect? What do you both stand to gain? This discussion is critical. It must be open, honest, and up-front. There is no need to say things in subtle, mysterious ways or to talk about unrelated topics to avoid confrontation or exposure. Both parties must know the expectations of the other. In this way, each will work toward satisfying the other. If one of the parties doesn't know the expectations of the other, there may be the belief that the expectation has been met, a belief that may be way off base. Therefore, write it down.

You may also have an executive who is very "me-focused" and doesn't even consider the other's expectations. The result will be a one-sided relationship – not by design, but by igno-rance. Don't expect people to know what you want – they don't. Don't be ashamed or afraid to discuss expectations or to ask for what you want. Not only is it OK, it is required. People don't know, even if you think they should. In like manner, don't presume to know what the other person expects. You don't. Even if they've told you what they expect, you will need to con-firm it periodically because things change. Even if both are very sincere in their endeavors to provide for the other, you must be sure you don't have a win-lose relationship. Unless corrected, win-lose will soon deteriorate into lose-lose. There are no ben-efits in lose-lose for either party. Therefore get everything out on the table and you can then deal with it. Some things are negotiable. Others are not. Know with certainty what is and what is not. Again, write it down.

Strategy

Strategy determines how the expectations will be accom-plished. What will you and your team have to do to give your executive what he wants? What people, resources, programs, investments, time, products, services will be needed? How will they become available? How can you do it with what's avail-able to you? Many issues will arise out of this. Cover these with your executive to make certain that the investments are seen as productive. He knows you have constraints. He also has preferences and is willing to forego certain things to get what's important to him. How will your expectations be met? What people, resources, investments, sales, introductions, information must be given to you for you to get what you want? This may be hard for you to ask for or discuss on the first attempt, but you've got to do it to take care of yourself and your company. If it doesn't look as though there is a way to get what you need or the chances are slim, it's better to know it up-front. Don't wait until you've done all the work and then find out there is no way you will get a win. Therefore, lay out the plan. What has to happen? Who will do what? What information is needed? What problems do we have and what can we do to solve them? What are the dates for getting things done? What will we measure to gauge our successes or shortfalls? Write it down.

Tactics

Tactics are what both you and your executive do to implement the strategy. One thing is to set up measurements and measure. Pay close attention to what's working and what's not. Take notes, assess, and interview people. Get people and programs moving to accomplish what has to be accomplished. Write down all the actions that have to take place and the dates that they will be completed. This is great to review as a measurement and it is rewarding to see tasks crossed off.

Communicate what's happening or not happening and get feedback, recommendations or whatever. In other words, work the plan. Make sure you understand what's happening. Adjust the plan when necessary and continue moving forward. Nothing should ever be a surprise. If it feels like its moving along in a boring way, then you know you're on the plan. You'll only notice the big change when you look back a few periods and see the change from then until now. The boring part is a big caution, however. Complacency sets in and the plans start to get ignored. Squeaky wheels start getting your attention. Greed to find other resources for fortune attracts you. You stop the attention to your executive. In the mean-time, your competitors are pounding away and "what have you done for me lately?" sets in. Boring on-going meetings and exchanges of information are good. Things are OK. Big revelation meetings are not good. They mean you've been out of touch and your relationship may be in jeopardy.

This may sound time consuming and over-whelming in light of all the other work you have. I realize this executive is not your only customer and you've got to do a thousand other things. However, it doesn't take extra time or effort. It only requires refocusing you attention and tasks. You just have to pay regular attention. Regular is what you both deem necessary. Stay in touch. Talk to other people for feedback. Most importantly, make a commitment for regular meetings and conversations with your executive. Schedule weekly phone calls, monthly visits, and quarterly reviews. Whatever it takes. Keep this thought in your mind: What would happen if this executive came to you one day and said he was going with the competition? How much effort would you then put-in to get it back? How impacted would you be by the loss of that relationship?

The Executive Relationship

The executive relationship is all about "What have you done for your executive lately" and "What has your executive done for you lately" – Win-Win. That's the bond. So, keep checking with your executive and with yourself. Does he/she see the value and feel happy? Do you feel happy? If not, it's time for a meeting to assess. Hopefully, it's not too late. Another thing to keep in mind is that competitors are constantly hustling your executives. And unlike a marriage, it's OK for the executive to leave you for the competition. There are few legal ramifications and it is socially acceptable. The only bond is results. So put a plan in place and keep implementing it, assessing the results, redoing it, and communicating. Keep attention on the plan. Then there won't be any incentive, time, or desire to listen to the competitors.

The journey to positive professional impacts will be enjoyable for your executive and you. The Beginning of Your Executive Relationships Starts Now. Sleep On It, and Make It Happen.

Workshop

Develop a plan for your best customer. Start it by yourself and write a date that you will complete this with a high level executive with whom you have a relationship.

TAKE ME TO YOUR
LEADER$